PRAISE FOR *LEADERSHII*

"Jon Singletary is a first-rate scholar of introspective leadership and how the Enneagram can help us lead and serve more effectively. *Leadership by the Number* helps all of us become more balanced in head, heart, and hand, and in doing so, to discover ways to lead from a stronger, more centered sense of self."

—*D. Michael Lindsay,*
President, Taylor University

"With cogency and vulnerability, Jon Singletary invites leaders toward the brave toil of understanding leadership as soulful work. His decade-long engagement with the Enneagram will inspire you to probe your self-awareness, generate collegial compassion, and elevate the effectiveness of your team."

—*M. Blythe Taylor, Assistant Provost for Integrative*
Learning, Barton College

"*Leadership by the Number* is one of the few Enneagram resources written with educational leaders in mind. My research has taught me that leaders are facing more challenges than ever before. *Leadership by the Number* equips leaders with self-awareness, compassion, and discernment to build more caring educational cultures in challenging times. This is a timely tool worth the investment."

—*Jorge Burmicky, Ph.D., Assistant Professor,*
Educational Leadership and Policy Studies, Howard University

"*Leadership by the Number* takes a fascinating approach to guiding educational leaders through the analysis of our individual Enneagram number to not only evaluate how it impacts our current practice, but also to identify how it affects our continued leadership growth and development."

—*April Willis, Ed.D., Principal Consultant,*
Forbes Coaches Council, Professional Speaker and Author

"What a delight to go on a deeper journey into the Enneagram with a guide as wise and kind as Jon Singletary! His candor, gentle spirit, and brilliant insights move us from appreciation of the Enneagram to life-changing applications."

—Todd Lake, Ph.D., Vice President for Faith-Based Engagement and Church Relations, Belmont University

LEADERSHIP BY THE NUMBER

LEADERSHIP BY THE NUMBER

USING THE ENNEAGRAM TO STRENGTHEN EDUCATIONAL LEADERSHIP

JON E. SINGLETARY

A Wiley Brand

Library of Congress Control Number.

Names: Singletary, Jon, author.
Title: Leadership by the number : using the Enneagram to strengthen
   educational leadership / Jon E. Singletary.
Description: Hoboken, NJ : Jossey-Bass, [2023] | Includes bibliographical
   references.
Identifiers: LCCN 2022059327 (print) | LCCN 2022059328 (ebook) | ISBN
   9781119880486 (paperback) | ISBN 9781119880493 (adobe pdf) | ISBN
   9781119880509 (epub)
Subjects: LCSH: School administrators—Psychology. | Educational
   leadership—Psychological aspects. | Enneagram.
Classification: LCC LB2831.83 .S56 2023 (print) | LCC LB2831.83 (ebook) |
   DDC 371.2/011—dc23/eng/20230208
LC record available at https://lccn.loc.gov/2022059327
LC ebook record available at https://lccn.loc.gov/2022059328

Cover Design: Paul McCarthy
Cover Image: © Shutterstock

SKY10043690_030223

*To my beloved wife, Wendi, and the ways the Enneagram
has shaped our relationship.*

CONTENTS

ABOUT THE AUTHOR

Jon Singletary serves as the dean of the Diana R. Garland School of Social Work at Baylor University. He has held the Diana R. Garland Endowed Chair in Child and Family Studies in the School since 2010 and first joined the faculty in 2003. Under his leadership, the school created an online MSW program that has tripled their enrollment and a multimillion-dollar research program that has contributed to Baylor's R1 recognition.

Dr. Singletary directed the Baylor Center for Family and Community Ministries where he helped lead $2 million of grant-related activities focused on congregational ministries that serve low-income communities. His research has focused on a range of Christian ministries, including family-based care for vulnerable children in Sub-Saharan Africa. More recently, his research has focused on Christian contemplative practices and the Enneagram as a tool for spiritual formation.

The focus of his academic leadership has been support for underrepresented populations at the staff, faculty, and student levels. Providing caring Christian community is at the heart of Baylor's mission, and he has led efforts to assure students experience that level of care.

Before coming to Baylor, he served as a Mennonite Pastor and a community organizer in Richmond, Virginia. Most important to his journey are the relationships with his wonderful wife, Wendi, a first-grade teacher, and his five young adult children, Haden, Raul, Harper, Ainsley, and Abbott.

ACKNOWLEDGMENTS

Suzanne Stabile gave me insights into my life and my most important relationships that I might have never seen otherwise. I had learned of the Enneagram in seminary and with friends as part of a beloved small group in our church. Suzanne took Wendi and me in as friends helping us move beyond the knowledge of the Enneagram to a place of wisdom as we saw our lives in new ways. I am grateful for Suzanne and the apprentice class that paved the foundation for this book.

The Garland School at Baylor is comprised of the most amazing colleagues who listened to workshop after workshop as new cohorts came to know their number and see themselves more clearly. I often say that I am not an Enneagram evangelist, but I will talk about it with anyone who is interested. Thank you for your interest, faculty, staff, and students, as friends who have come to value this resource for self-awareness.

Across our university, colleagues have come to appreciate the Enneagram. There is a rich and diverse array of Enneagram communities on our campus. I am grateful for the interest in it that has been expressed by the President's Council, Student Life, Athletics, Development, Human Resources, and almost every division on campus. President Linda Livingstone and Provost Nancy Brickhouse have supported my leadership and I am deeply grateful for their own. Baylor is a special place, seeking to be faithful in our missional commitment to being a top-tier Christian research university.

I am particularly thankful to one of the outstanding students who became my graduate assistant, XiXi Brinkhuis. XiXi created all of the artwork in the book and on my social media. She helped edit and shape ideas and she has flourished as a compassionate social worker who values the Enneagram as a tool for her own professional growth.

The team at Jossey-Bass has been phenomenal. They have held my hand when needed and given me freedom to run when desired. Ashante

Thomas, Pete Gaughan, Mary Beth Rosswurm, Barbara Long, and Tom Dinse helped me gain new insights as a writer and have been so supportive each and every step along the way.

I would not be anywhere close to the teacher, writer, and consultant I am today without Meghan Becker's presence in our family. Meghan and her two daughters, Ellie and Sarah, have been at the heart of our journey through life together for over a decade. Meghan teaches with me, has helped form several Enneagram community groups, and reminds me of the value of story that makes the Enneagram come alive for people. Our story together helped make this book possible.

Finally, I would like to convey my deepest gratitude to my family. I appreciate the beauty of my family even more because of the ways the Enneagram has helped us see and celebrate one another. As a result, our love and commitment to each other continues to grow through the best and worst of times. Haden, Raul, Harper, Ainsley, and Abbott are the most beautiful gifts. They inspire me. They keep me on my toes. They are proud of me. And I am so proud of each one of them. I love you dearly.

And none of this would exist without my beloved and beautiful wife. Wendi, thank you for loving me. For teaching me. For treasuring me and our relationship. You remind me that our love is rare and to be cherished. We have learned that over and over again. And the Enneagram helps us not take any of it for granted. I love our energy together and how we make our way through life. Thank you for engaging this tool to help us see the beauty of what we have so clearly.

INTRODUCTION

I did it again. Just last week, I caught myself in a meeting, my fourth Zoom meeting in one day, and I was in charge. I was blowing through the agenda, already thinking about the next meeting. And I realized I was making a decision based on how I would be perceived. I worried how the decision would be a reflection on me and I worried about how it would then reflect on our academic program. I did want the best for our school; however, I realized I was making a decision that was as much about me as it was about us. I get busy or overwhelmed and my automatic response is to protect myself from failure.

What are the things you do over and over, without meaning to, things that get in the way of your desire to lead well? I know I am not alone. Your struggles will be different than mine, but they are there. Maybe you also want to be seen as valued. Or needed. Or competent. Maybe you want to make sure you will not be betrayed. Make sure you get it right. Make sure you are safe. We all have automatic responses to the demands we face as leaders. And they show up again and again. In meetings you lead. In hallway conversations. As you avoid certain interactions. Can you see yours?

These automatic responses show up when we are busy or overwhelmed. When we are not grounded and intentional, not present in the moment. But being present in the moment takes a lot of work. And did I mention how busy we are?

Educational leadership incorporates the wide range of competencies we seek to develop related to facilitating excellence in teaching and learning and nurturing high quality teaching and learning in our educational systems. It incorporates mentoring and empowering colleagues to strengthen their teaching and learning practices. It seeks to address and improve educational policies, resources, and systems. And it promotes scholarship to improve educational outcomes. In all of these tasks and responsibilities and the many more we can identify, we know that, as leaders, there is a great burden to perform, grow, and improve at every turn.

So much of our focus as educational leaders is on the external demands of leadership. We are responsible for important decisions about important things. We are responsible for other people, and their well-being. We are balancing budgets, supervising staff, and juggling competing expectations. Most of our work as leaders is on influencing and improving the world around us and the people in it.

And yet, despite these external opportunities and demands, I am convinced it is the internal work that is of utmost importance. We long for guidance and support in these and other essential functions, but we must learn the value of looking within. We have to understand our core values and what motivates us. We have to understand how other people affect us as well as how our own internal struggles affect us. What is the story we tell ourselves about how we lead, what works for us, and why we fail?

As educational leaders, we have one essential resource that we must nurture and develop—our sense of self. We must learn that to strengthen our inner identity as a leader we have to turn within. We must learn to lead from the inside out. We often hear about the importance of self-awareness, but we seldom learn the skills to practice it.

The internal journey of self-awareness is key to the change we desire as leaders and the Enneagram can be a helpful tool to guide us in this work. This book introduces the Enneagram as a resource for self-understanding as well as growth and transformation. The Enneagram is an ancient symbol that identifies nine ways people function in the world, often thought of as personality types, and each of the nine is shaped by our capacity for feeling, thinking, and doing.

Learning to wake up to our sense of self, to practice self-observation, requires us to understand the role of feeling, thinking, and doing as three dimensions of leadership. The Enneagram helps us learn to see these characteristics within ourselves and to balance the way they function in our lives. We all have the capacity to feel in connection with others, to think through the relevant information available to us, and to do the work that is required of us as leaders. However, we are each predominantly driven by one of these three dimensions and we have one that requires significant development. Can you begin to see how these three function for you? How they shape your leadership?

This book will guide you on this journey: to learn to see yourself more clearly, to learn about the Enneagram and identify your primary Enneagram type, and to learn how the three dimensions above shape the ways you function as a leader.

BY THE NUMBER

What does it mean to do something *by the number*? The phrase is an early American military reference to learning how to follow orders. It is comparable to doing something by the book, to doing something in a formulaic, predictable manner.

Do you see the ways your responses as a leader are formulaic and predictable? You may not, but chances are other people see the formulas that shape you and that they can predict some of your behaviors better than you can. You may not want to hear that you are that mechanistic in how you lead. And, of course, we do have the freedom to grow and to change—but first we have to see the patterns that get us in trouble.

We do have the freedom to make choices about how we want to live on a daily basis. Or do we? Theologically, I believe in our free will to make decisions. Psychologically, however, there do seem to be some constraints on our behaviors. If I am awake, self-aware, consciously engaged, then I can freely choose many things in the course of any given day. However, I too often function on autopilot. I operate in a mechanical and even predictable manner. The subconscious and unconscious parts of my identity drive my decisions in ways I do not see or understand. If I can learn to see these things at work, then I can respond differently. First, we have to learn to wake up.

These habitual patterns of our personality shape us in ways that keep us operating *by the number*. Mechanically. Habitually. Unconsciously. According to the Enneagram, there are nine common patterns shaping how we function. These nine types describe how we commonly operate, how we make our way through life when we are not awake and fully engaged.

We too often operate according to our personality. By the number. According to our dominant Enneagram type. But, we can choose to live consciously, freely, from a more balanced perspective rather than being driven by our personality.

What does it take to live this way? To identify our Enneagram type? To find balance in our life?

It begins by learning to see. Observe your emotional responses that can overwhelm you and learn to identify the feelings that underlie them. Recognize the ways you are stuck in your head rather than having an open mind. Sense the gut reaction that instinctively drives you and learn to act intentionally. To learn to feel, think, and do more freely is to live from your soul. To develop an open heart, open head, and open hands is to live out of the essence of who you are.

It sounds so simple, but learning to see yourself this clearly takes work. It takes time and it takes patience. A Scottish neurologist and Enneagram teacher we will learn about in a later chapter, Maurice Nicoll, is instructive here, "Remember that you do not change by being told what to do. You only change through seeing what you have to do when you realize what your being is like." He continues, "All our theories on improving the world, while we are still asleep, merely intensify the sleep of humanity" (Nicoll 1996).

Are you ready to wake up to the patterns of your personality? To the ways you have fallen asleep to your own patterns of living and leading? The Enneagram will be our guide in this work. It will help us see ourselves more clearly and offer insights to how we might lead in new and different ways.

In this book, we will look at the foundation of the Enneagram, the psychology behind it, and the spirituality that undergirds it. As I have mentioned, each of us subconsciously prioritizes feeling, thinking, and doing differently, and the result is nine patterns that make up the nine Enneagram types. This book details how these patterns work for each type and how to bring these dimensions into balance. My belief is that making sense of the ways thinking, feeling, and doing function for better or worse in your life is central to becoming the leader you are being called to be.

You may already know your Enneagram type, or you may be learning about the Enneagram for the first time. If you do not know your number, there are resources here to help you begin to identify it. If you already know your number, this book will add an additional dimension to what that means for you. For each of us, this book will help us learn how to use the knowledge associated with our Enneagram type to develop more fully as a leader.

The chapters in Unit One introduce the three core dimensions of who we are and how these feeling, thinking, and doing capacities work within us. We will see how learning to live with these in balance is a way to strengthen our capacity for leadership. In learning the structure of the Enneagram, I will introduce the triads and stances and also provide an introduction to each of the nine types. The focus here is more than simply learning our number; it is learning how our number fits in this larger system that can help us see ourselves with greater clarity as we seek to lead.

Unit Two goes more in depth with the Enneagram triads and stances, and how the three dimensions are stacked within our personality. Which one drives our personality? This question points to our Enneagram triad. And which tends to be the greatest struggle for us? This points to our Enneagram stance. Seeing the internal structure of our personality, the triad and stance for our core number, invites a deeper level of self-reflection and this is the first step in nurturing growth and change as a leader.

Unit Three brings a practical approach to the stances, in particular, and to finding balance in the three dimensions that shape us. The application here is presented as stancework, and observing, listening, and allowing are the tools for growth to help us nurture open hearts, open heads, and open hands. Resources related to mindfulness are essential Enneagram practices for growth as a leader. My hope is that this book will provide some of the skills to guide us inward so that our outward-focused leadership reflects the value of the leaders we long to be.

UNIT ONE

People everywhere are talking about their Enneagram number. For too many, it is an excuse we use for bad behavior or a weapon we use to criticize others. The Enneagram, however, is designed to be a resource for self-awareness, a tool for helping people interested in a more meaningful journey to better understand themselves. How do we reclaim the value of this ancient resource?

We begin by seeing how the Enneagram is a tool for self-reflection. So much of our focus as leaders is on the external demands of leadership. We are balancing budgets, supervising staff, juggling competing expectations, and making big decisions. We long for guidance and support in these and other essential functions; however, as leaders, we have one essential resource that we must nurture and develop—our sense of self. We must learn that to strengthen ourselves we have to turn within. We must learn to lead from the inside out. We often hear about the importance of self-awareness, but we seldom learn the skills to practice it. The internal journey of self-awareness is key to the change we desire as leaders, and the Enneagram can be a helpful tool to guide us in this work.

Unit One introduces the Enneagram as a resource for self-understanding that leads to growth and transformation.

The Enneagram is an ancient symbol that identifies nine ways people function in the world, often thought of as personality types, and each of the nine is shaped by our capacity for feeling, thinking, and doing.

We begin with these three core dimensions of human functioning and why they matter to our development as leaders. These dimensions are inherent to understanding the Enneagram, and they show up in various leadership disciplines and in most theories of personality. They are elements of our personality we all use all the time, but when we slow down and consider what they mean, we can pretty easily notice the extent to which our leadership is lopsided because we rely on one of these more than the others. Our leadership is likely more thinking-oriented and data-informed, or maybe it is more feeling-focused and relationship-based, or perhaps more doing-dominant and task-centered.

In addition to these elements, I invite us to look at other elements that shape the nature of the Enneagram as well as some of the history associated with it. The symbol itself is made up of nine points around a circle, and I introduce the nine personality types associated with each point.

As leaders, we know we have as much to learn from our struggles as our strengths, and the Enneagram helps us see both sides of who we are. The elements of struggle in our personality can help us more clearly identify which of the nine types is at our core.

From there, we can learn how the other points on the Enneagram relate to our type. Namely, the wings and arrows make up other numbers around the symbol that are also part of the inner working of our personality.

In all of this, learning to look within to develop a stronger sense of self-awareness is the goal. Leadership comes from within, and the Enneagram helps us see that. It is an invaluable guide for the inner work that is required if we want to be more effective in the outer work that we associate with leadership.

CHAPTER ONE

HEART, HEAD, AND HANDS

The Core Dimensions of Human Potential

God, I open my heart to you. Fill me with your love.

I begin with the words I utter each day as part of a spiritual practice. I call it practice because it takes a lot of work to make myself sit still, and to do so regularly. It takes just as much work to allow myself to be open to the power of love within me. As a dean, as a husband, as a father, and in most areas of life I know, I benefit from these efforts to experience the divine within, but it is an effort.

Perhaps it shouldn't be this difficult. I grew up knowing that I am loved unconditionally. However, I also grew up with a belief that I had to work to accomplish being loved. In my head, I knew I was loved. I could agree to this idea. I could see that it was true in the lives of the people around me; these were some of the most tender, loving, and kind individuals. And yet, I always struggled to internalize the belief that I am loved simply for who I am.

As a leader in my school, I know I am valued. I know my team members respect me. I know they love me. We truly have built a phenomenal community of nurture and support. We lead an organization where people feel heard and where our commitments to each other and to our shared work flow from a place of care and connection. And yet, I wake up most Monday mornings filled with anxiety. I worry about the work. I worry about the team. I worry about my connections. Am I there for them? Am I taking the time to listen? To build them up? Am I leading in a way that reflects the beloved community we desire?

What makes my morning mantra even more significant for me is the fear of how I project my negative belief onto others. I so strongly feel that I must work hard to be loved and I just assume everyone feels that way. I made my way through teenage and young adult years pushing myself and everyone around me to work harder. I never said the words "work harder so that you can be fully loved," but it was what my head told my heart, and so my hands were always hard at work, hustling for love. Even today, a commitment to silence and stillness is essential in order for me to hear the voice of love.

To know we are loved requires that our heart, our head, and our hands work together. However, this is rarely the case for any of us. For me, it was more difficult to feel loved; for some, they can't wrap their mind around it, and for others, they don't believe their actions will ever matter enough to be able to embody love.

ELEMENTS OF THE SOUL

I have worked my entire career in higher education in a religious context. While Christian teachings shape much of how I understand myself and my work, I am always interested in other religious traditions and spiritual practices as well as other disciplines and fields of study. The three dimensions of heart, head, and hands show up over and over again in writings about personality and leadership, but before we say any more about them, I want to highlight the spirituality of these concepts; in other words, I want to share how my own beliefs and practices have shaped my understanding of these things. These three dimensions are at the core of what I believe about who we are as human beings, about how God has made us and how God is creating us still. These three dimensions can be described as the core of the human soul. I begin with this religious reference, but shift to discuss the soul as a symbol for our human potential. I make references to the idea of soul growth. While this is in part a spiritual concept, it is often used in Enneagram writings as a metaphor for our ability to be our best self.

In the Christian scriptures in the book of Mark, someone asks Jesus what commandment in the law is the greatest. Jesus said, "You shall love the Lord your God with all your heart, all your soul, all your mind, and all your strength. And the second is like the first, love your neighbor as yourself."

Jesus's response to the simple question "Which of the laws is the greatest?" leads us on the lifelong journey of learning to love ourselves, our neighbors, and our God with the wholeness of who we are. Wrestling with each of these dimensions of who we are—heart, soul, mind, and strength—continues to be worthy of our exploration, particularly as we seek to fulfill the second command, to learn to love the people around us and to better love ourselves.

In this, Jesus highlights loving God with our heart, using the word *kardia,* which is what we think of as a common reference to the source of all feeling. He points to the head, or *dianoia,* translated as "mind" or "the source of our thinking." And he points to the hand, or gut, from *ischus,* translated as "strength" here, but also "power," "force," or "ability," which are all references to the instinctual doing center of our bodies. Feeling, thinking, and doing show up in how Jesus explains the command to love God.

This verse references the word translated as "soul," *psyche,* which is the unique human dimension that makes us who we are. We often say that the soul is intimately connected to our spirit. Spirit and soul play a role in the fullness of who we are, as innate characteristics that animate who we are as humans.

None of these functions can be fully separate apart from the others, so why is soul not in the common and frequent references to heart, mind, and strength? One way of understanding the connection is that the soul is the fullness of who we are when the other three dimensions work together. The soul functions as a fourth dimension, or better yet, as a collective understanding of how heart, head, and hands work in tandem. Modern psychology, also from the word *psyche,* talks about the existence of the other three as centers of human functioning that shape our personality. Theologically, we can talk about the soul as the way in which each of these other three elements function together. That is to say, the heart, head, and hands function together as core dimensions of our soul.

The health of our soul, and our health as a leader, we will see, is found in balancing our capacity for feeling, thinking, and doing.

Paying Attention to the Soul

We often hear that finding balance in life is essential. It requires slowing down and that just seems impossible sometimes. A dear friend of mine, the Rev. Julie Pennington-Russell, once asked: "Does the velocity of your life exceed your ability to be present?" Absolutely mine does. And if my speed isn't problematic, my focus is. With the goal of seeking to be effective, I never slow down and I am chasing too many things at once.

In a similar vein, my Enneagram mentor, Suzanne Stabile, teaches that the pace of our lives and our focus outside of ourselves lead us to a place where we easily lose the ability to observe the imbalance in our lives, and as a result, we lose touch with the value of the soul. This part of her Enneagram teaching builds on the work of Carl Jung as well as George Gurdjieff. It is a classic truth and remains a modern problem for too many of us. As leaders, we never slow down. Busyness defines us. The pace of my hurry keeps me from staying centered in the notion that I am loved, that I have innate value. It keeps me from being present to myself as well as my colleagues. My focus on all that is coming my way keeps me from being centered within my heart, my head, or my hands. My life keeps my soul out of balance and always on the run.

Another pastor friend of mine, Rev. Mary Alice Birdwhistell, shared an African story of 19th-century European missionaries who were making their way from one Sub-Saharan village to another. They hired local porters to help them make their way. On day one, the porters moved at a slower pace than desired and so on day two the missionaries took the lead. At the day's end they went twice as far as they had on day one and were proud of their leadership. However, on day three, the porters refused to continue the trip. The missionaries asked why they were not moving and the local leaders, from a place of balanced wisdom, replied, "We are waiting on our souls to catch up."

As a leader, when I am pushing for the data I need to justify my rationale for a big decision and not listening to the stories of people's lives, my soul has to catch up. When I only trust my gut despite the data and the factors around me, and force things to go my way, I have lost touch with my soul. When I worry about how people feel about me rather than making the decision that is needed, then my soul is out of balance.

One more religious teaching highlights the importance of the soul, this time from the Hebrew Bible. The beginning of the 23rd Psalm reminds us of God's desire to restore our souls: "The Lord is my shepherd; I shall not want. He makes me lie down in green pastures and leads me beside still waters. He restores my soul."

Balancing the Three Centers for Soul Growth

Balancing how you live and love with your heart, head, and hands is the path to balance in our soul, to restoring our soul. It is the path to soul growth. Soul transformation. Soul healing. Growing your soul is essential work for this journey. Becoming whole, becoming the person God intended us to be and is creating us to be, is soul work, and soul work requires paying attention to the role of feeling, thinking, and doing on our spiritual journeys.

Poet and Novelist Kurt Vonnegut offered a group of students some advice in an open letter:

Practice any art, music, singing, dancing, acting, drawing, painting, sculpting, poetry, fiction, essays, reportage, no matter how well or badly, not to get money and fame, but to experience becoming, to find out what's inside you, to make your soul grow. . . . Seriously! I mean starting right now, do art and do it for the rest of your lives. (Usher 2017)

Then he gave the students an assignment:

Write a six-line poem about anything, but rhymed. Make it as good as you possibly can. But don't tell anybody what you're doing. Don't show it or recite it to anybody. . . . You will find that you have already been gloriously rewarded for your poem. You have experienced becoming, learned a lot more about what's inside you, and you have made your soul grow.

Growing your soul may be a new to us way of thinking about the work of leadership development, but it is not new. The late 19th-century Russian mystic George Gurdjieff and his colleague, early 20th-century Scottish psychiatrist Maurice Nicoll, wrote about "the work" of a Fourth Way spirituality—a way that incorporates the three dimensions of head, heart, and body as the pathway to a fourth spiritual dimension, the soul.

Gurdjieff left behind very few writings about his teachings. Nicoll describes Gurdjieff's work as learning to see what lies within us as a way to foster change: "The movement of this Work is psychologically inwards, at first. Later it is both inwards and outwards." From Gurdjieff, Nicoll focuses on the need to wake up from a state of inner sleep, of being asleep to our personality. He says, "Life makes us identify with the personality. It naturally makes us identify with what it has itself created in us. The Work is to make us cease to identify with what life has created in us and is now doing to us" (Nicoll 1996).

For Nicoll, being asleep to personality means being asleep to the mechanical reaction of our three centers, our intellectual center, our moving center, or our emotional center, as he described these dimensions within us. To awake from this sleep, we must practice self-observing, or self-remembering. He describes how we each have "some fixed attitude that we are entirely unaware of." And challenges us, "If you remain in inner darkness, how can you proceed? Whoever we are, we find ourselves, through self-observation, possessed of a certain small number of typical ways of reacting to the manifold impressions of incoming life. These mechanical reactions govern us." On the other hand, "if you awaken to being, if you change your being, your life changes."

In the mid-20th century, Bolivian philosopher Oscar Ichazo and Chilean psychiatrist Claudio Naranjo expanded ideas from the teachings of Gurdjieff and Nicoll. They also each drew on ancient sources, the Christian desert father Evagrius Ponticus and Greek philosopher Pythagorus of Samos. The Enneagram, shown in Figure 1.1, is the common thread of their work, a resource for understanding the soul, and for understanding the intersections of psychology and spirituality within us (Quirolo 1996).

By the 1970s, Naranjo was popularizing Gurdjieff's, Nicoll's, and Ichazo's ideas about three dimensions at work within us. He also noted that there are three ways of ordering and arranging the three dimensions

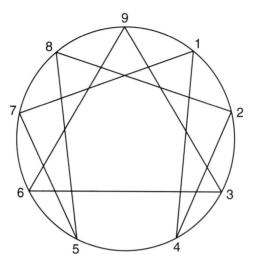

FIGURE 1.1 The Enneagram.

of feeling, thinking, and doing that result in nine pathways or personality types that shape our spiritual development, our psychological formation, and our soul. The result is the modern Enneagram movement where nine personality types are built around the three dimensions (see Figure 1.2).

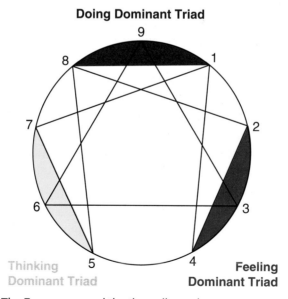

FIGURE 1.2 The Enneagram and the three dimensions.

Kathy Hurley and Ted Dobson (later he changed his name to Donson) best describe the earliest intention of the Enneagram as it relates to these ideas: balancing heart, head, and body is a lifelong journey, and it is the only way to "discover your soul's potential" (Hurley and Donson 2000).

THE THREE CENTERS OF INTELLIGENCE

The ability to balance feeling, thinking, and doing is what makes humans unique; it is what gives shape to our soul. Furthermore, we see references to these three dimensions show up in all kinds of times and places, in various disciplines of study and different professional fields.

Most commonly, these ideas have been referred to as three centers of human intelligence, noting that the human brain has an affective, cognitive, and instinctive function. That is to say, we not only have a thinking brain, we have a feeling brain and a moving brain. Some have said that within the brain, the frontal cortex is the thinking center, the amygdala is the feeling center, and the hypothalmus controls the body's urges. Jerome Lubbe uses functional neurology to talk about the instinct of the brain stem, the intuition of the right hemisphere, and the intellect of the left hemisphere (Lubbe 2020).

Others argue that the enteric nervous system comprised of our gastrointestinal organs or the entire autonomic nervous system in the core of our body function as a gut-driven, action-oriented brain, that the heart and central nervous system function as an emotional brain system, and that the cortex of the brain itself is home to our mental processes. While the science of three brain functions is still developing, we can easily recognize that humans have a core capacity for these three dimensions and that our ability to feel, think, and do makes us unique.

To explain these three characteristics figuratively, we often use the bodily symbols of heart, head, and body. Or, for alliteration with heart and head, hands can be used as the symbol for doing, for instinct, instead of body or gut. We know a heart person as a feeling-oriented person. Someone in their head is a thinker. A trust-your-gut, hands-on kind of person is someone who follows the instincts of their body to get things done.

Feeling, thinking, and doing are so commonly understood as intelligence systems because they are each relevant to so many aspects of life. They shape our understandings of physical and mental health, organizational well-being, and leadership development. At times they work together; more often, they work apart to influence any number of actions and decisions we make. In psychological terms, these three ideas are known as emotional (feeling), intellectual (thinking), and instinctual (doing) centers of human functioning (Heifetz and Linsky 2002). In classical personality theory, and fields such as the psychology of personality, we hear about a person's patterns of thoughts, feelings, and behaviors, another similar way of describing the same concepts (Allport 1960). And in leadership, a little background research can help highlight several theories and models that emphasize the importance of paying attention to these three elements that make us who we are. Let's turn to some of the research in leadership fields related to education, business, and religion before defining the three dimensions from the perspective of the Enneagram.

The Three Dimensions in Educational Leadership

The three dimensions of feeling, thinking, and doing show up in a wide range of disciplines. Here, we consider what these mean in education, seeing them referenced in literature related to primary, secondary, and higher education, in theory, practice, and research.

Robert Roeser posed a central question confronting 21st-century education:

> How can we better educate young people today not only in the academic skills and knowledge they need to succeed as workers in the global economy (e.g., the head), but also in the social-emotional, ethical (e.g., the heart) and practical skills (e.g., the hand) that they need to flourish and to be engaged citizens who can help address the pressing global challenges of our times? (Roeser 2020)

With the Teaching Lab, Adrienne Williams offers a specific model of teacher preparation focused on education equity. This nationally known nonprofit has established an evidence-based model of professional learning that they call Head, Heart, Habits, and Equity. This culturally responsive model seeks to ensure that underserved students meet educational outcomes by developing great teachers. Their model states that the head addresses core academic content and research-based approaches to teaching, the heart focuses on teaching communities that nurture social capital and empowerment, and habits are the repeated, structured classroom practices they promote. Finally, equity is included as the goal of the first three elements of their model (Williams 2020).

In the field of adult education, transformative learning theory incorporates critical self-reflection and meaning-making in the "a-ha" moments of life. The model's creator, Jack Mezirow, presented the theory as a largely rational process with a focus on cognitive understanding of our experiences (Mezirow 2000). Kevin Pugh created the transformative experience theory to measure three characteristics of transformational education: expanded perception (cognitive, or head), expanded value (affective, or heart), and active use of learned concepts (psychomotor, or hand) (Pugh 2011). Edward Taylor demonstrates that the focus on making meaning in one's environment and the importance of community in this work suggests an affective dimension (Taylor 2017). This tension between the head and the heart is found throughout the writings on transformational learning.

One additional approach to transformational learning is built on an understanding of the impact of all three of the centers and is entitled the "head, heart, and hands model for transformational learning." Julia Singleton highlights the head as a cognitive domain relevant to critical reflection, the heart as an affective domain relevant to relational knowing, and the hand as a psychomotor domain relevant to engagement (Singleton 2015).

From an Indigenous American approach to transformational learning, Alaskan Unangan educator Ilarion Merculieff together with Libby Roderick write, "Learners are expected to use their inherent intelligence to figure things out on their own. Inherent intelligence includes the physical senses (hearing, touch, taste, smell, and sight) and the senses of the mind and heart (intuition, gut feeling, emotion). When these senses are all active, the answers can come from within." Body, mind, and heart work together for the sake of holistic learning if we can recognize the value of the three intelligences that operate within us. Merculieff and Roderick continue to describe how traditional and Indigenous cultures teach us that learning is located in the entire being, including the brain, the body, and the heart. "We act more authentically and fully when we utilize all our gifts and senses. Combined, these gifts and senses 'see' more than if we just used our brains. We need them all in order to become real human beings with a deep sense of connectedness to All That Is" (Roderick and Merculieff 2000).

The Three Dimensions in Business Fields

In business, we see the need for attention to these three core elements show up in a variety of specialized fields, from marketing to management. Business scholars utilize these dimensions to ask how customers respond to markets. A 2015 issue of *Harvard Business Review* featured "Think, Feel, Do" on the cover. An article from marketing consultants Arons, van den Driest, and Weed describes the "ultimate marketing machine" comprised of three fundamental business principles: to think is to utilize data and analytics to build insights, to feel is to understand consumer engagement through their drives and perception, and to do is to engage customers in a total experience and the associated production work (Arons, van den Driest, and Weed 2014).

Specific to management and organizational leadership literature, adaptive leadership is a field focused on "whole leaders" who utilize "three brains" of leadership: head, heart, and gut. This follows the work of *New York Times* journalist Daniel Goleman and TalentSmart founders Travis Bradberry and Jean Greaves on the importance of "emotional intelligence" for leadership development, where emotion can be used to inform thinking and behavior in our environments (Bradberry and Greaves, 2009; Goleman, 1995).

Grant Soosalu and Marvin Oka created "mBraining," which uses "mBIT," multiple brain interaction techniques, to help leaders align and integrate head, heart, and gut for increasing a sense of self-understanding in our leadership (Soosalu and Oka 2012). They have continued their research, which highlights how decision-making involves not only cognition, but also emotion and intuition, forming a three-factor research model of these concepts.

Organizational research also focuses on cognitive, affective, and instinctive dimensions of well-being. Corporate executives and scholars David Dotlich, Peter Cairo, and Stephen Rhinesmith published *Head, Heart, & Guts*, which focuses on leadership development in several corporations where learning to balance these principles is emphasized, including Bank of America, Johnson & Johnson, and Novartis (Dotlich, Cairo, and Rhinesmith 2006).

The Three Dimensions in Religious Leadership

In a classic argument on these dimensions at the intersection of religion and psychology, Ken Pargament discusses spirituality as how people think, feel, and act in efforts to experience the sacred in our lives (Pargament 1997). Similarly, Father Richard Rohr returns us to the theological foundation of the centers, "We need each part—body, heart, and mind—fully engaged to live as our most authentic and loving selves" (Rohr 2013b).

Finally, educational leader Dennis Hollinger, author of *Head, Heart & Hands: Bringing Together Christian Thought, Passion and Action,* addresses the same concepts from the perspective of Christian spirituality:

Head, heart and hands all play a significant role in our Christian faith. Our minds, passions and actions interact in such a way that unless all three are present and nurturing each other, we are less than the people God created us to be. To be whole Christians, head, heart and hands must join together as joyous consorts. (Hollinger 2005)

Heart, head, and *hands* are the words I will use for these three centers, or dimensions, that shape us and contribute to our well-being, to our self-understanding. Gurdjieff and Nicoll named these functions the intellectual center for head, emotional center for heart, and instinctive-moving center for hands. Some use mental, emotional, and physical. I have simplified the names of these centers to feeling when talking about the heart, thinking for the head, and doing for the hands.

DEFINING EACH OF THE THREE DIMENSIONS

Having seen the three elements show up in various fields of study, what do we know about how these characteristics shape us in our own lives? What do we know about each of these characteristics on their own? And, what do they mean in terms of our own leadership?

Let me define these dimensions for us. As part of this, I also want to introduce how they relate to the Enneagram's personality types. I will say more about the Enneagram and each of the nine types in the next chapter; here, I only highlight how the numbers are arranged in relation to the three centers. You may not know anything about your number yet. Before we get there, I want us to become more familiar with these three dimensions. Regarding the numbers, there are three types that are dominant in their use of the feeling dimension, three in the thinking dimension, and three in the doing dimension. We call these three groups of three Enneagram triads.

At the same time, there is another grouping of the nine Enneagram types, known as stances, that I discuss in a later chapter. While the triads are most obvious since these groups of three are easily categorized together and represent a dimension that is dominant within our personality, the stances are the opposite. The stances represent a dimension that is repressed within our personality. None of us balance all three dimensions perfectly, and by default, one of the dimensions is dominant in our personality and one is repressed. For example, a feeling dominant, feeling triad type is a Four; the Four is also doing repressed. That is to say they are people who are connected to feelings, and they often have deep thoughts about their feelings; being able to do something about these feelings and ideas is a common challenge for a type Four.

Feeling

Feeling is the core function of our heart-based dimension. The feeling dimension has to do with relationships, with being aware of the connections we long for, the needs we have, and the needs of others. This dimension includes emotional responses; however, emotions are an external expression of feelings, which are inner understandings of the needs we have and that we sense in others. Feelings are the conscious recognition of what underlies our unconscious emotional responses. The next time you have a strong emotional reaction to something, see if you can sit with it and recognize the deeper feelings associated with it.

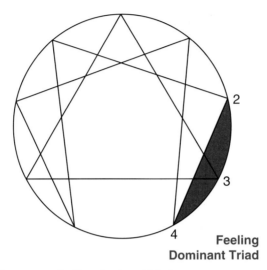

**Feeling
Dominant Triad**

FIGURE 1.3 Enneagram feeling dominant triad.

From the perspective of the Enneagram, the feeling dominant, heart types are the Two, Three, and Four (Figure 1.3). People who identify with one of these Enneagram types are often most in touch with a sense of what feelings mean and how important they are to human relationships. At the same time, they can be so heart-centered that their feelings overwhelm them. These types are feeling dominant, but being dominated by feelings is not always ideal. We call these three the heart triad, or the shame triad.

While three types are heart dominant, there are also three types who tend to trust their heart the least, or who struggle the most to connect to their own feelings or the feelings of others. These are the Seven, Eight, and also the Three; we call these three who focus on their intellect and instinct, rather than emotions, the assertive stance.

Did you see that the Three is in both the heart triad and assertive stance? What does it mean for them to be driven by feelings, but to also struggle to connect with their feelings? They are the type most likely to worry about how people feel about them, but find it most difficult to really feel their feelings or genuinely tune in to the feelings of others. More later on the assertive stance and the place of the Three within it.

The Feeling Dominant Triad

A close friend, a case manager for students on campus, is a Two. She has some comfort level with her own feelings and emotions, but she has a much greater focus on the feelings of others. She will set aside her own needs for hours at a time to listen and ask in-depth questions about life, love, loss, or whatever the people she is with are feeling in the moment.

I identify as a Three. I am an academic dean, trained as a social worker and a minister; I know the value of feelings, but it takes a lot of work for me to listen intently to anyone talk at depth about their feelings. And yet, at the same time, I spend most days worrying about how people feel about me! It is a twisted approach to feelings, and one I have to work with in order to see. Few of us who are Threes are as adept at living out of our hearts as we believe ourselves to be.

When talking about feelings, a student who identified as a Four talked about lighting candles, creating space for her emotions, and sitting down to revel in the feelings behind them. Is that you? I like the sound of that, the image of it, but I am never patient enough to do much more than buy the candles that I think I will use for such a practice!

Thinking

Thinking is the core function of the head-based center. Its work is focused on logic and analysis, reasoning and rationale. Processes such as planning, evaluating, and analyzing are common in our use of head space. Thinking is about gathering information—data—and using it to make plans. Thinking is of great value for all of us, but none of us use the capacity of our head to the fullest. Some of us are reluctant to trust what is in our head, and some of us cannot get out of our heads. A thinking dominant person may tend to overthink things, though they may not see it that way.

Thinking dominant Enneagram types are Five, Six, and Seven (Figure 1.4). This does not mean these are the smartest types (no offense, Fives!). It does, however, mean that they start in their head as a default response to life. In a crisis situation, they take it all in through their need for ideas and information, their capacity to think and make sense of the situation. We call these three the head triad, or fear triad.

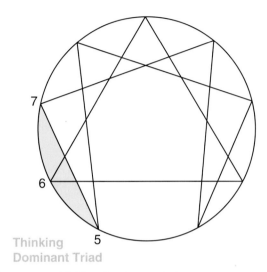

Thinking
Dominant Triad

FIGURE 1.4 Enneagram thinking dominant triad.

While these few types start with their head, there are also a few types who innately trust their head response the least. They may be every bit as intelligent as the head dominant types, but they function as thinking repressed. They trust others more than their own thinking and may depend on others for reassurance. They also trust their gut response or their heart connection more readily than their head. These are types One, Two, and Six, and we call them the dependent stance.

You will notice the Six is in both the head triad and dependent stance. What does it mean for them to be thinking dominant and thinking repressed? They are the type most likely to need information to feel safe and supported, but the least likely to trust the information they have. More in a later chapter on the dependent stance and the place of type Six within it.

The Thinking Dominant Triad

On the introverted side, a faculty colleague is a Five. She is a collector of information and ideas, but is much less likely to share them with others or even engage in conversation about them unless she knows she is prepared in her responses. She has deep thoughts about her feelings, she knows the difference between feeling and thinking, and she is much more concerned about being competent and overcoming a sense of worry about her loved ones than being a feeler who is concerned with image and how others feel about her.

I work with another colleague who is a deep thinker, a Six, but she would only reluctantly describe herself as a thinker. She worries about her security and that of her family. She is a strong feeler, but she knows she spends more time in her head and is prone to overthink things in far too many situations. She is great at asking questions, but is much more hesitant at confidently understanding and stating her own beliefs.

An alumni friend who is driven from this perspective is a Seven and she lives her life thinking about life's dreams and the endless possibilities they present. She had "dreamer" tattooed on her wrist before learning she was a Seven. She can rationalize anything and loves an energized exchange of big ideas.

Doing

Doing is the core function of the hand-based center. It is focused on action and what can be accomplished, or more importantly what can be controlled. The result of being led by our hands is a high level of reflexive motor functioning, or instinctive, physical responses to daily situations where others may respond with thoughts or feelings rather than action. We tend to know the difference between doing and the other two functions. However, the function of the hands is not just getting things done. The hands are for accomplishing tasks, but they are also a symbol for that physical, natural, instinctual drive to act, apart from what the heart or head would suggest.

The doing types of the hand triad are the Eight, Nine, and One (Figure 1.5). They are driven by their bodies, or their hands, and this doing orientation includes a strong desire to be in control of their situation, of what they are doing and how they do it. They trust their gut, and following its lead is what drives them. When they realize they cannot be in control of every situation and when others challenge their instinctual drive, it leads to frustration or anger, leading this group to also be known as the anger triad.

Likewise, there are three numbers least driven by a doing orientation, and they struggle to find the energy needed to follow through or engage all the demands of life. These are the Four, Five, and Nine. Sometimes this means people who identify with these numbers want to do things their own way at their own pace, and sometimes it means they want to

Doing Dominant Triad

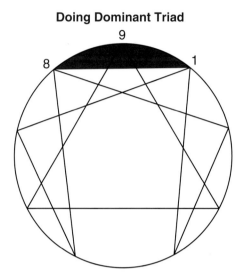

FIGURE 1.5 Enneagram doing dominant triad.

step away to avoid the tasks at hand. As a result, these three are doing repressed and are known as the withdrawing stance.

The Nine is the type who is doing dominant and doing repressed, or in the hand triad and withdrawing stance. This means they may sense the need for someone to act, but do not assume it is theirs to do. They know priorities matter, but it takes a lot of energy to follow through. I will say more about withdrawing stance types in a later chapter.

The Doing Dominant Triad

A fellow leader on campus talks about knowing what to do in her gut. She is an Eight. She trusts her gut to guide her and it seldom lets her down. Like most Eights, she is in constant motion. There is always something that needs to be done—often in the form of a challenge that needs to be taken on.

A fellow leader on campus who is a Nine is also aware of his body guiding him; he just doesn't trust that his actions are as meaningful, and while he feels the need for action, he's content to ponder the possibilities in a way that seems less hands on. He may look like a thinker or a feeler, but he is always weighing the energy his decisions require and how doing what needs to be done might matter, questioning if he's the person to get it done.

Another friend with a similar personality talks about having fidgety hands, hands that need to respond, not a mind that needs to think about it or a heart that needs to feel. This friend is a One, and one difference is her internal motivation to do what is right. She is almost as active as my Eight friend, but in a different way with a constant worry about the integrity of her actions.

This chapter offers some initial insight into the core dimensions of our human experience as well as how these dimensions serve as the foundation for what have become known as the nine Enneagram types. The Enneagram is almost always introduced in terms of these three elements, but rarely are we given an opportunity to explore the meaning of these parts of ourselves apart from our number.

There is much value in understanding that the core of our leadership is grounded in the health of our soul, and the health of our soul is rooted in the balance of these three dimensions and not only in understanding the dominant center of our personality type. When a discussion of our centers is grounded only in triads and learning our dominant center, we assume we have one of these dimensions mastered and the other two are not as important. In time, we will learn that balance of the three is central to the transformative leadership experiences we desire. The journey begins with seeing which dimension is most central, but continues in learning that our dominant center can get us in as much trouble as the other two. Learning to balance all three really is key to our growth as leaders.

I have briefly introduced the nine Enneagram types here in relation to our three core dimensions. In the next chapter, I turn to the structure of the Enneagram. I say more about the role of the three centers, how the modern Enneagram came to be focused more on the nine types, and a reminder that while the three dimensions and your specific number matter are core to using the Enneagram, the connections we have to other numbers also help pave a way for the health of our journey.

CHAPTER TWO

THE STRUCTURE OF THE ENNEAGRAM

I stepped into the role of academic dean in a season of deep personal and professional grief. My academic mentor and our dean, Dr. Diana Garland, was diagnosed with pancreatic cancer in spring 2015 and passed away within months. While I was serving in the role as interim dean, my own mother's cancer grew worse. She passed away a year after my mentor, leaving me to figure out how to lead our school through our collective grief while wrestling with my own. Dr. Bonnie Miller-McLemore, theology professor at Vanderbilt, described my experience in this season as "the beautiful anguish of vocational liminality," the thin space of in-between what has been and what is yet to be, the daunting and yet common place of uncertainty that frequently comes our way.

Wrestling to feel my feelings while leading our school in this season was not easy. Seeking to balance feeling, thinking, and doing put me on a renewed path seeking to engage the inner work of leadership. Authenticity with such experiences is what I desire as a leader, and what so many of us long for, but can be such a challenge.

During this season of grief, I found some old Enneagram notes reminding me that "transformation always follows a simple path, not a complicated one" (Hurley and Donson 2000). This is among the first teachings I read by Hurley and Donson over a decade ago as I was being introduced to the Enneagram. "Growing our soul" as they describe it is really a simple matter of learning to quietly look within ourselves. The sadness, the desire to lead well, my own grief and that of my colleagues—there was so much to carry, and sitting with my feelings was pushed to the bottom of my priority list. Walking in the liminal space certainly didn't feel like a simple path of transformation.

Nothing is more difficult for me as an academic leader than making the time to simply and quietly look inward. When I first read this teaching several years earlier, I was a newly tenured associate professor and director of a faith-based research center. I was making a living by complicating the spiritual life. My doctoral dissertation and subsequent research focused on religion and politics (nothing simple there) and I was taking steps toward academic leadership.

I was working in my head as a theologian and I valued the work of my hands as a social worker addressing social justice. I was all about what I could accomplish as a social work academic, but discerning vocation meant making sense of what was happening in my heart. I had not yet developed my mantra of opening my heart to God and asking to be filled with love, but that is what I longed for.

Hurley and Donson taught me to simply look within to experience the work of soul growth. They taught that we spend most of our time and energy focused outward, engaging the world around us and struggling to find our place in it, and we spend very little time focused inward, on the spiritual journey, the journey of the soul.

They taught that these three dimensions of who we are as humans can be nurtured as part of this inner work, and these dimensions can be balanced to work together to make us whole; this is soulwork. We typically are not engaged in the inner work of the soul and we live most of our lives driven by one or two of these dimensions in an externally focused way. We let our personality take over. We follow its lead, rather than questioning our ego self and asking if our soul may be oriented another way.

What does this look like? Some of us try to make sense of the world in our heads, trying to understand how it all works. Others of us are in our hearts trying to connect the relational dots. And others follow the path of our hands, holding tightly trying to control each step as well as the results. As I mentioned in the first chapter, one of these paths is dominant for each of us and it shows up in our leadership as we catch ourselves making decisions and guiding others without stopping to be present and aware. We experience this in the behaviors that drive us in our family life, where the patterns of how we engage our partner or our children are more habitual than we may realize. And, we do this in our spiritual life, staying in our head to understand God, or in our heart seeking a stronger relationship with God, or by our hands, trying to be in control of our life and God's place within it.

In patterns such as these, or maybe other behaviors where you recognize your personality at work, the Enneagram can be a simple guide, although its many layers make it seem more complicated than needed. In this chapter, I introduce the Enneagram by revisiting the three dimensions at its core and how those shape the nine ways we make our way through life. Many have given helpful introductions to the Enneagram types, so I will summarize the nine types by their triads and focus on what Ichazo and Naranjo described as the passion and virtue for each type. Some authors present the passions as the sin or addiction of each type. My goal is to help us understand these characteristics as a psychological and spiritual resource for each number.

THE THREE DIMENSIONS OF THE ENNEAGRAM

At the beginning of the 20th century, George Gurdjieff began to collect ancient spiritual teachings and added his own understanding of the spirituality of this symbol. In his eclectic teachings, Gurdjieff talked about three specific spiritual paths. One path is the path of the heart, for those who emphasize the role of feeling and connection on our faith journey. A second is the head path, for those who seek knowledge and insight of understanding of the divine. The third path is the path of the gut or body, the instinctive drive to move us toward God. The fourth way is what Gurdjieff described as the way that made the most sense to him, a way that balances each of the three and is the way of the soul. This, of course, is the most difficult path.

Moving between the three dimensions and moving around the nine points of the Enneagram is symbolic of the movement of God within us. Gurdjieff had much more to say about this movement around and within the Enneagram rather than about the nine points. He also focused more on the importance of the three dimensions working together within us to make us whole. Just as it takes three strands of hair to make a braid, it takes each of the three dimensions to make the soul healthy and whole. These kinds of analogies were the heart of his teaching on the Enneagram.

As Enneagram teachings continued to develop, three types emerged for each of the three dimensions of the Enneagram and the organizing structure that emerged for these groups came to be known as Enneagram triads. The heart triad is comprised of the feeling dominant numbers, Two, Three, and Four. People who belong to this triad may not realize how feeling oriented they are, and being led by the heart does not necessarily mean these numbers are the best feelers on the Enneagram; just that the desire for connection and relationship drives them.

Likewise, those in the head triad of thinking numbers, Five, Six, and Seven, may know that they operate in the world by taking everything in through their brain first, but they don't see just how dominant this need to analyze and understand is in their personality. People who identify with these numbers may be wise and insightful, but that does not mean they are the most intelligent; however, their mind is what drives their way of being in the world.

Doing dominates the hand triad, Eight, Nine, and One. People with these personalities are driven by their bodies to be physically engaged. This does not make these types the most productive or the most aware of their body, but we often see them for their energy and how active they are.

The placement in the Enneagram of each of these triads related to heart, head, and hand is shown in Figure 2.1.

The triad approach follows the Enneagram around the circle neatly pointing to three heart types, three head types, and three hand types, highlighting the types dominant in their feeling, thinking, and doing. There is another way to organize and present the number that focuses on which of these three dimensions is the biggest struggle for each type, or which dimension is repressed by their personality. Just as the heart dominant numbers are driven by feelings, there are three types who struggle the most to connect with their own feelings as well as the feelings of others, the Threes, Sevens, and Eights. Similarly, three types tend to be less confident and connected to their head and the role of thinking in how they engage others, the Sixes, Ones, and Twos. The third stance group wrestles with how to engage their body, with doing what they think needs to be done as well as with what others expect of them; these are Nines,

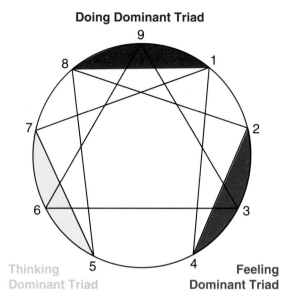

FIGURE 2.1 Enneagram with three triads.

Fours, and Fives. This grouping of numbers, shown in Figure 2.2, is known as the Hornevian Groups (based on the teachings of feminist psychologist Karen Horney), the social styles (based on the work of Don Riso and Russ Hudson), or Enneagram stances (based on the work of Kathy Hurley and Ted Donson).

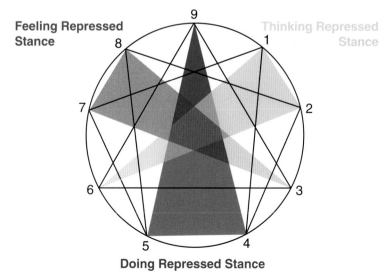

FIGURE 2.2 Enneagram with three stances.

Learning to see within yourself the extent to which one of the three dimensions is dominant and also the degree to which one of them is a struggle for you is an essential process for Enneagram awareness. The next two chapters provide more insight into the triads and stances, painting the picture of how the personality of each number is structured in terms of feeling, thinking, and doing.

While these three dimensions can help us better understand the inner working of our personality, the Enneagram is most helpful when we can identify our type and explore the depths of each of the nine ways we are shaped. Moving from the three dimensions to the nine types is comparable to moving from a color wheel of the primary colors of red, yellow, and blue to seeing all the colors of the rainbow. The spectrum of the rainbow is comprised of seven distinct colors, and yet each is a combination of red, yellow, and blue. In my teaching, I use a small box of Crayola Crayons—there are only eight, and I wish Crayola added one more for my Enneagram analogy! However, we can see that the eight colors give more diverse options for our coloring projects than having to only use the primary colors, and yet they all result from combinations of red, yellow, and blue. The Enneagram, likewise, is a symbol of nine ways of being in the world, and each type, each approach to life that shows up in our personality, is a combination of a person's capacity for feeling, thinking, and doing. Figure 2.3 highlights the nine types using variations of

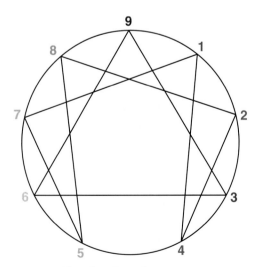

FIGURE 2.3 Enneagram with colored numbers.

red, yellow, and blue to demonstrate the variety of personalities captured by the Enneagram and we will return to these colors throughout the book.

THE NINE ENNEAGRAM TYPES

A Bolivian teacher, Oscar Ichazo, and a Chilean teacher, Claudio Naranjo, expanded Gurdjieff's ideas about the Enneagram's three dimensions to focus on nine characteristic patterns of personality. They discovered how nine distinct personality types can be organized around the three dimensions of heart, head, and gut. Gurdjieff taught the Enneagram as a process-oriented symbol to help us understand the inner processes of feeling, thinking, and doing at work within us. Ichazo and Naranjo were the first to teach about nine distinct ways these processes are at work and to talk about these as nine distinct personality types (Labanauskas 2021).

When Naranjo talked about the nine "Enneatypes" he described nine "character structures" with passions being the emotional problems of our personality and fixations being the mental flaw, both seen as deficits in terms of how we understand ourselves. From the Greek word for "engrave," *charaxo,* or character, is what Naranjo uses to describe "what is constant in a person because it has been engraved upon us, and upon our behavioral, emotional, and cognitive conditionings." In other words, the very nature of how we go about feeling, thinking, and doing on a daily basis is engraved in our enneagram personality type. This engraving is what others have called an addiction, a vice, a sin, a suffering, and what Naranjo says is "an emotional passion associated with a cognitive fixation"—a personality that gets us into trouble and keeps us there (Naranjo 1994).

The effect of our passion is as an addiction, an intense, consuming emotional energy, a compulsiveness that defines the very nature of our personality. Ichazo made clear that to understand better our passion, we also need to understand virtue. Each Enneagram type has a chief virtue, characteristics to which we long to return. We can, and do, live out all nine virtues, but one virtue is at the core of our path back to God, to the essence of our identity. Our personality, however, forces us to focus on our addictive passion instead of our virtue (Ichazo 1982).

What does this mean? Ichazo taught that, as a Three, I was born for the virtue of truthfulness, or authenticity, a desire to live out my true and beloved self, but instead I learned to live out of my passion, my core sin, which is vanity. I truly learned early on in life that it is so much easier to settle for vanity, to try to prove my worth with charm and trying too hard to convince people I am a great leader. This performing and achieving personality was easier than learning to embody my true, authentic self. The Enneagram has helped me realize just how accurate these things are for me, which helps me know I am a Three. For me, looking for love by seeking success is a matter of looking in the wrong place and it distracts me from being authentic with my anxiety and desire for approval.

Naranjo describes this common human experience of living our false self rather than our true self with a story about a man looking for something in an alleyway. A friend joined him in the search for what he learned was the missing key to his house. After a long while the friend asked, "Are you sure you lost it here?" The man replies, "No, I lost it at home." "Then why are we looking here," the friend answered back. "There is more light here to help us look," the man said.

So it is with our Enneagram passion and personality: we are looking for the key in the wrong place. We are looking for fulfillment. We are looking for purpose. Naranjo says we are looking for the person God is calling us to be, but we look outside ourselves rather than within.

Similarly, Gurdjieff said we are looking for the essence of who we desire to be. Because of our distinct passion, however, we are each looking in the wrong place. I will not find it by seeking to prove my value. You will not find it by being helpful. You will not find it by overexerting your need to always be and do what is right. You will not find it by having the right information, by being in charge, or by understanding yourself. And you will not find it by questioning everyone and everything in an attempt to be prepared or by avoiding everyone and everything in an attempt to keep the peace. These are the nine ways we wrestle given our Enneagram type.

The following Enneagram figures are adaptations from what Ichazo learned from Gurdjieff, making it more distinctly focused on nine passions of our personality that lead us away from our best self, shown in Figure 2.4, as well as nine virtues that lead us back to our best self, in Figure 2.5. In addition to these, Ichazo created over 100 additional Enneagrams, which he called Enneagons, to help flesh out the characteristics of nine distinct ways we live and make our way in the world.

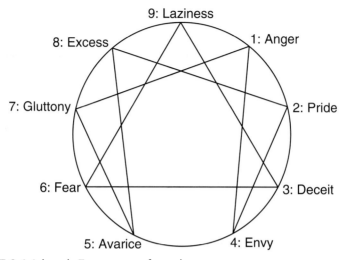

FIGURE 2.4 Ichazo's Enneagram of passions.

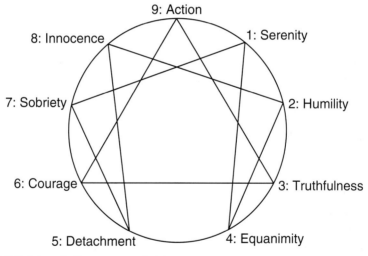

FIGURE 2.5 Ichazo's Enneagram of virtues.

The Importance of Discernment

Based on these characteristics from Ichazo, Naranjo saw several habitual patterns of personality begin to emerge. These Enneatypes are not based on behaviors so much as on the underlying, unconscious motivations that drive our emotional, intellectual, and behavioral patterns, the patterns we see as personality.

People immediately want to know how to identify which of the nine types reflects their individual personality and understandably they ask: Where do I take a test to figure this out? The Enneagram itself predates psychological testing of personality. The earliest teaching associated with the symbol assumed a process of discovery of one's type rather than a test telling us. Over the years, several tests have become available, each with different levels of reliability and validity, or consistency and accuracy, in typing us.

You can find several tests online and maybe a test can help you discover your type; however, most of us who teach the Enneagram describe learning one's type as a matter of self-reflection and discernment. Slow, deep listening is how we learn to see ourselves clearly and Enneagram work is primarily about learning to see ourselves more clearly. Listening to our lives, "letting our life speak," as Parker Palmer puts it, is a simple task, not a complicated one, but it is one that takes patience and focus, dedication and commitment (Palmer 2000).

I often tell students that if they would take the test and sit with each question for a day, journaling about their responses, then Enneagram tests would be better tools for discernment. Instead, the tests ask us to answer quickly without overthinking our responses. Sometimes that first response is best and most accurate; however, sometimes, it can take a while to understand who you are, what motivates you, and why.

How would you respond to the following prompts, not on a scale of agree to disagree, but with a two-page journal entry?

- I am comfortable with confrontation.
- I tend to be more relationship-focused than goal-focused.
- I typically engage feelings before deciding on a response.
- I tend to have questions and need more information when making decisions.
- I prefer to maintain social distance and remain independent.
- I worry about how others perceive me.

Taking a test may give you the most accurate understanding of your Enneagram type, but not necessarily so. There are many Enneagram tests and some are better than others. Regardless of what test you might choose to take, I always return to the importance of discernment in identifying your number. What is your life teaching you about yourself?

In learning to listen deeply and in looking for your number, you are not choosing your idealized self, not who you want to be. You are looking for an authentic description of who you are most of the time, of how others likely see you across contexts, from work to family to time alone. Likewise, try to identify the characteristics that most hold true over time— how you understand yourself now, and how you were in your twenties, when our personality, for better or worse, is at its strongest. It is those late adolescent and early adult years when you have tested a sense of identity and developed a sense of self. As lifelong relationships develop and we begin to mature in new ways, we all tend to create a sense of balance and rub off some of the rough edges of our personality. However, it is often the struggles of our personality that help us identify our type, that help us see ourselves most clearly, even if most painfully. Can you see the ways your personality is at work?

Identifying My Type

To help you begin to identify your type, I am going to provide a brief introduction to each number. I share a reflection on how each type approaches work and leadership and ground the description in Ichazo's and Naranjo's original teaching on the passion of each number as well as the virtue. The passion is usually more obvious within us and it highlights a struggle that keeps us from being grounded, mindful, or truly present to the opportunities that lie right before us. However, it does take some time spent in self-reflection to identify this characteristic passion within you.

Richard Rohr teaches us "the goal is not to get rid of our passions" (Rohr 1995). Rather, the point is to embrace this shadow side of our core strength and to see it more clearly for what it is. Furthermore, overcoming this passion is not just a matter of will. We must embrace it, offer ourselves compassion, observe what we can in how it shapes us, and then trust the value that comes with it. Rohr suggests that once we can observe the passion of our number that we learn to hold it, observe it, and trust the best part of it. We can also remember Hurley and Donson's teaching: "All the negative qualities of your number are but distortions of this pattern's strengths and positive qualities" (Hurley and Dobson 1991).

To help us on the path of recovering our virtue from the influence that our passion holds over us, I incorporate Rohr's teaching about the distinct path of each type. This path that each of us takes based on our personality is the misguided path for discovering who we long to be (Rohr 1995). It is akin to looking in the wrong place for the key that brings meaning to our life and leadership. Can you identify your passion, the path you are taking, and the virtue you long to recover? Can you use these introductions to the nine Enneagram types to identify which is your core type? As I present this introduction to each number, I include the core passion or struggle, the core virtue that can bring balance to our personality, and a path, which is a way of thinking about the transformative growth opportunity to help us on this journey.

Ones: Anger to Serenity and the Path of Improvement

"If it's the right thing to do, it's the right thing to do," says a One responsible for an internship program in our university.

Ones in the workplace are diligent and hard-working. They are purposeful and principled. Ones want to follow the rules, and integrity is a value to which they are wholly committed. They are committed to what is right and they cannot imagine that anyone would not be. While they are open to input, they are sensitive to critical feedback; they are already their own harshest critic and are frustrated when others correct or criticize them.

Ones don't describe themselves as angry, because anger is not a good thing and more than anything they desire to be good. However, Ones are frequently disappointed, perhaps frustrated with themselves or dissatisfied with their sphere of influence because things are not the way they should be. They are driven to work for change, to fix things, because of how things are. Ones may be angry at you, but they are far more likely to be angry with themselves for not measuring up; they have an internally focused anger with a desire for principled responses and purposeful self-control. With awareness, they can find their way to serenity, a calm inner peace that quiets their body as well as their head and heart.

As leaders, Ones have a desire for reform in the workplace. They value focus and clarity, honesty and integrity. While they may be critical, they are driven toward what is good and right, and are compassionate and supportive leaders. When centered, they can calm the inner critic and find a path to improved performance without a need to control all the details.

Twos: Pride to Humility and the Path of Relationship

"How it makes people feel is as important as the decision itself" says a Two leader in academic affairs working on curriculum changes.

A Two is a positive and encouraging person who nurtures relationship and values being supportive in the workplace. Saying no and setting boundaries can be difficult for a Two. Twos want to please people and strive to win them over. Being kind and considerate is important to them, and so is being liked by others. They want to be seen as a helpful person and they are often able to anticipate the needs of others.

In fact, Twos need to be needed by others, and yet they struggle to recognize their own needs. They struggle to see their own pain and doubt others love for them. How can you learn to see in yourself what you see in others? Not seeing your own needs is your pride at work. Twos are not cocky; they are loving, kind people who want to nurture, help, and make others happy. They seek approval from others and desire to be loved by giving so selflessly and denying their own needs. In becoming aware of this overreaching attempt to connect, and knowing their help is not needed by everyone, they can find the virtue of humility.

In leadership, twos are empathetic and emotionally focused. They care about the feelings of others and the need to respond to those caring perceptions. They are generous and sensitive to others. They long to be helpful, loving people and in leadership, balancing the demands of a leadership role with the weight of relationships is always a challenge. Twos often define themselves in terms of relationship. Learning to find their center in themselves requires finding their value apart from others as deeply as the value they bring to others. They must learn to see that they need us as much as we need them.

Threes: Vanity to Authenticity and the Path of Work

"I'm glad that's done. What's next?" remarks a Three who serves as an administrator in student life on our campus.

Threes are competitive and driven at work, and in most areas of life. They have a sense of what needs to be done and the drive to get it done well. They want to be seen for their achievements and work hard to succeed in all they do. Looking successful is what often matters most and being real requires an emotional awareness that feels overwhelming. Driven by effectiveness and efficiency, they find little value in feeling their feelings.

Threes often believe that everyone is presenting an image that they can do whatever is needed in an effort to prove their value. Expressing genuine feelings gets in the way, so they set feelings aside in order to focus on a desired image of success. They exude confidence and positivity, yet behind the smile is an honest doubt about their worth. When they become aware of their vanity in thinking that they can always impress others in order to feel valuable, they experience the virtue of authenticity.

Threes are natural leaders, driven to accomplish desired goals and focused on vision and strategy. They think big and know how to implement. They are task-oriented, but they are also self-conscious. They know how to succeed, but they worry about failure. Becoming a workaholic is a risk many Threes face in seeking to prove their worth. People know what Threes can accomplish; Threes must find their value in stillness as much as they do in their productivity.

Fours: Envy to Equanimity and the Path of Beauty

"I don't think people know how hard this is. And if they do, how do they just keep going?" This is from a Four who works in student affairs.

In the workplace, Fours wrestle to find their place and to make sense of it. They want to fit in and they want to stand out. They want to be happy and they feel like the world is too much. Fours compare themselves to others, focus on the depth of their experience, and analyze the meaning of their connections. They desire authentic expression, they are sensitive, and they value their emotions. They pay attention to what is missing whenever there is the potential that they may be misunderstood.

When Fours focus on what is missing, they are not envious of things that you have, but rather they feel an intense desire for something lacking in their sense of connection. They are always comparing, wondering how people seem so happy, so emotionally settled when their emotional lives are a roller coaster. When they become aware of this passion of envy, they see that they are looking for more and comparing themselves to others. Seeing this opens their eyes to the virtue of equanimity, which is emotional stability or calm.

Fours are not looking to lead in a traditional sense, but they do long for what is beautiful and unique to inspire them. They often lead by longing: until we are set apart by X, we will never have Y. They bring a distinct intensity to their work and a desire for creativity in their tasks. It is only in realizing the beauty and value of what they have, rather than what they long for, that they find a meaningful way forward in their work.

Fives: Avarice to Nonattachment and the Path of Knowledge

"I walk into a classroom and we are discussing philosophy and I know I belong here. I am competent here and I can relax. I walk into a different classroom and I keep my head down, try not to be seen, and cannot wait for it to be over." A graduate student reflects on being a Five.

Fives often prefer to go life alone, which takes less energy; this is how they approach work as well. They do not want to be dependent on anyone for anything. They want to step back, taking the time to understand and figure things out. Fives need time and space for privacy so they can focus on making sense of the world around them. They are curious and have ideas for how to improve things for the better; however, their tendency to observe rather than participate means they hold onto what they know until they have to share it.

Fives long for more knowledge and hold tightly to the knowledge they have. This tight grip reflects their passion of avarice, or greed. They are not greedy for things, but for the privacy to develop the knowledge to feel more competent in the world. When they become aware of their struggle to hold on too tightly to what they take in, and the fear of opening up to others, they can see that they have been withholding from the rich experiences of life with others. In becoming aware of the gift of connection, they find the virtue of nonattachment, or generosity with their ideas and their energy.

Fives have a need to know more in order to trust that they can lead with confidence. Their journey to understand and make sense of the work around them takes as much energy as the implementation of the tasks required to accomplish their goals. As a result, Fives hold on to what they know rather than sharing it freely. They can find ways to foster connection and share the vast resources they have as they lead others.

Sixes: Fear to Courage and the Path of Loyalty

"Cautiously assertive, but secretly not 100% confident," is how a community leader who is a Six describes herself.

At work as at home, Sixes value connection and the security relationships provide them. They check in with the people they trust, asking questions to offer guidance. Sixes work hard, value others who do as well, and will likely wonder what might go wrong. They will analyze a situation trying to make a rational decision, even if it takes extra time to do so. They are kind and compassionate, loyal and dependable.

Sixes value loyalty because they need people to offer support and help them feel secure. But it is difficult to trust people when they also doubt themselves. They want to be prepared for any scenario and pitfall, so they ask questions and doubt the information they have been given. When they become aware of this passion of fear, they can see that they are trying to find something secure to rely on when the virtue of courage is already within them.

Sixes can find and support an inner confidence to lead a team in meaningful ways. They may be fearful of how to get to that place of confident knowing, or they may doubt themselves as they seek to implement their plans. Trusting others matters, but learning to trust oneself is even more essential to the tasks of leadership.

Sevens: Gluttony to Sobriety and the Path of Freedom

"That's so exciting! I can't wait!" exclaims a Seven about a new class they get to create.

Work that allows innovation and excitement appeals to Sevens. They value freedom and flexibility and are drawn to what is new and energizing. Sevens are positive leaders and will reframe negative experiences into something positive. Sevens like having a range of diverse opportunities at work, but none that require too much long-term attention to detail. Having to focus on details or being asked to do the same thing over and over quickly turns off a Seven.

Sevens want to experience everything. They are always anticipating the next adventure in life. Too much is never enough; hence, the passion of gluttony. They think a variety of options is needed to find satisfaction in life. When they become aware of this passion, they can see that they are focused on the future possibilities of life instead of what is real, here and now. This recognition introduces them to the virtue of sobriety, a meaningful and aware presence, a satisfied heart.

As leaders, Sevens appear fearless. They trust in their ability to take care of themselves and their desire for more options, more choices, and more freedom distracts them from the inevitable limits of life. They seek to escape the emptiness and the pain of life; the true freedom to lead effectively comes in resting in what surrounds them.

Eights: Lust to Innocence and the Path of Control

"Go hard or go home," one nonprofit leader writes about herself.

Eights work hard and they are decisive. They want others to be as well, and if that is not the case, they are able to step in and take charge. They don't feel the need to lead, but they won't let anyone cause their project to fall apart. Eights are strong and direct, and they always believe there is a way to accomplish what is needed. Eights don't always know their own strength and are surprised to hear they may be intimidating to colleagues.

Lust is how we describe the passion of the Eight. Lust is about intensity, and eights move with passion, force, and conviction. Only the strong succeed and they believe they must assert themselves to be in control. When they become aware of this passion that is truly passion, they see how assertive they are in striving to protect themselves. With awareness, they can then experience the virtue of innocence, an inner strength and a childlike surrender to the desire for control.

Eights lead with intensity and vigor, with a desire to be in control of what is happening to them. They will let others lead, if they believe they can trust them. Eights do not need to control others; they just don't want to be controlled by them. They do not want the results of another person's leadership to negatively affect them. Trust and vulnerability may come at a cost; however, such surrender allows even greater outcomes in their work with others.

Nines: Resignation to Engagement and the Path of Harmony

"Why would I want to assert my way?" asks a Nine leader about his role at work.

Nines adapt in order to maintain a sense of peace. At work, they can help others do so. They are effective mediators and facilitators, who are able to see every side of an argument and remain patient with others. Nines can be indecisive and slow to act, focused on minimizing conflict in all they do.

The passion of a Nine is often labeled sloth, but sloth is not laziness; it is resignation, or avoiding the energy required of life in hopes of avoiding conflict. However, sometimes avoiding conflict creates conflict. Minimized internal attention to their own feelings and needs leads to minimized response to external forces. They long to remain unaffected by life in order to live in harmony with everyone around them, and in waking up to themselves, they can recognize the cost of resignation. From this, they can develop an openness to the virtue of engagement or action, a response that they can learn is worth the energy.

Nines do not ever want to lead in a way that is perceived to be aggressive or ambitious. Not believing their voice or presence matters, it is easy to go along in an effort to get along. Active engagement may bring conflict, but it will also bring the full presence of a Nine in leadership, and that is what every organization needs.

I hope this overview grounded in the passion and virtue of each number gives you some insight to what your number might be. Before you rush out to take an Enneagram test, spend some time reflecting on each type description to see which characteristics reflect your way of being in the world. Can you narrow it down to two or three options? Or, are there some you can rule out? Much like a physician testing symptoms to rule out certain medical conditions, you can likely rule out certain types that are least like you. Perhaps then you can identity two or three that could possibly be your core type. Sit with each of these for a little while to see which feels most consistent with how you see yourself and how you think others see you. If you still are not sure, be patient with yourself and the process of discerning your type. This is central to the work of the Enneagram.

FINDING YOUR TYPE

Finally, if you just can't stand making sense of it without more certainty, feel free to try one of the following Enneagram tests. But remember, they may not be absolutely correct in what they identify as your type. You know yourself better than the test will know you.

Enneagram Tests to Consider:

- Wagner Enneagram Personality Style Scales (WEPSS)
- Riso and Hudson Enneagram Type Indicator (RHETI)
- Integrative Enneagram Questionnaire (IEQ9)
- Truity Enneagram Personality Test

With an idea of what your core number might be, let us consider how other elements of the Enneagram can be instructive for our journey.

I said at the beginning of this chapter that authentic transformation follows a simple path, not a complicated one. It may seem that explaining the structure of the Enneagram and figuring out your core Enneagram type are awfully complicated ways to navigate a simple path. It is true that the Enneagram can easily become complicated. It is an ancient symbol shrouded in mystery. It is a puzzle of three groups of three, and within it are several other groupings of three. And it takes time to understand yourself in one of the nine types.

We have to identify one of the nine types as our core number, and that number reflects an inner psychological struggle. While these characteristics are attempts to explain the complexity of who we are, they can also help us see the simple functions of our capacity for feeling, thinking, and doing. These simple, perhaps oversimplified, dimensions for understanding our sense of self are really the core of the Enneagram journey. Before returning to these dimensions, let us take another look at the structure of the Enneagram itself, and the numbers we often refer to as our wings and the numbers across the arrows from our core number.

CHAPTER THREE

THE FLOW IN AND AROUND THE ENNEAGRAM

Wings and Arrows

M.C. Escher's artwork invites you to stay engaged as you try to make sense of all the different directions it goes at the same time. "Relativity" is one of his most beloved pieces, and Kylie Brooks of the Brigham Young University Museum of Art describes it as "a series of staircases [that] crisscross in a labyrinth-like interior" (Brooks 2018). The picture has one person going up and in the same plane on the same staircase someone else is going down. One person is looking down over a balcony and another is looking up at the same view from the same floor. The stairs overlap and connect in ways that can be overwhelming.

Working with a challenging student is always a struggle for me and can make me feel like I'm traversing Escher's staircases. I recently started a semester with the challenge of upholding academic standards while also offering flexibility in light of the coronavirus's impact on our learning. One student, in particular, remained frustrated with my approach. My sense of failure in trying to connect with her tanked me in week one. What's worse is that it made me want to overcompensate and prove my worth in other ways. When I cannot win a student's approval, then I will really strive to prove my value in another class or with colleagues. I will go overboard to show just how successful I can be.

But then, I can also just check out. I can feel deflated, and nothing is as appealing as tuning out. I wonder how quickly I can get to bed for the night as I wish for a fresh start to a new day.

I know my job is not about winning students' approval. And I know that after 25 years of teaching, I should know better than to let someone else control the joy I feel in my work. And yet, I find myself feeling like I am climbing one of Escher's staircases. I'm trying to climb up, but feel like I am going down. One moment I was looking across the horizon from a high point and the next I feel like I am underneath it all looking up.

The sinking feeling I had in this moment and in reflecting on Escher's artwork mirrors the dynamic nature of the Enneagram. As I saw these different temptations begin to rise up this week, I realized I was preparing to teach about movement within the Enneagram and I had a perfect example with my own experience.

THE DYNAMIC NATURE OF THE ENNEAGRAM

The *Enneagram of process* can be said to describe Gurdjieff's approach to this ancient symbol and what it meant to him. For him, the Enneagram was a tool to help us wake up to our personality, but he never talked about nine personality types. He did focus more on the three centers or dimensions of mind, heart, and body, and the transformational journey of seeking to balance these elements within ourselves. This process was focused on learning to "wake up" as he encouraged his students to wake up when we are asleep to the illusions we have about ourselves given how difficult it is to see the habitual patterns, or passions, of our personality.

The *Enneagram of personality* is the next step that Ichazo and Naranjo offered to the symbol and this work, focused on nine distinct types, but still grounded in the three dimensions. As part of this, Naranjo also contributed the idea of Enneagram wings and arrows to show that there is still a process focus in and around our personality types. While the nine types are a clear step away from Gurdjieff's process Enneagram, the movement of our number between our wings and across the lines does help explain the dynamic process of our personality as it shifts at different times and in different situations.

I am among those who believe that your core Enneagram number does not ever change, but the fact that we do experience growth and shifts in our personality that point to other numbers within us can be explained, in part, by the wings and arrows. As a Three, I can relate to my Two and Four wings. The wings are simply the numbers on either side of your core number and they rub off onto your core number. These numbers shape what makes you unique in your expression of your core number. I am a Three, but I always have a little Two and a little Four at play in my personality. My wife, an Eight, always has some Seven and some Nine influencing her. Some of us are more aware of our wings than others, and some have stronger wings than others. Some rely more on one wing than the other, and some experience a shift from one wing to another over life's journey.

Likewise, the arrows follow the lines across from our number to two other numbers that also influence our core number. Naranjo referred to these numbers as having to do with situations of stress and security, and while these concepts are pretty common among Enneagram teachers, Peter O'Hanrahan, in the Narrative Enneagram tradition, talks about the lines as dynamic points representing a more significant shift in our personality. The changes that come from these arrow numbers bring different behaviors, different ways of seeing ourselves, and different ways of interacting with others. These connections are more relevant in helping us grow in our personality and helping us expand our understanding of ourselves in a way that leads to transformation. He describes how we have access to a whole new set of resources "[that] create needed balance to our usual personality. Moving to these dynamic points can help us step out of the box, expand our options, and become less stuck" (O'Hanrahan 2019). Rather than focusing on which arrow is stress and which is security, which is a resource point or which is a relaxation point, I simply suggest that both numbers across the arrows have something to offer your personality as sources of growth and healing.

As a Three, I know the ways I connect to Nine, one of the numbers across from me, because I sense it most days. I am on the go all day, but at the end of a long day when the demands of work have piled up (because Threes don't set limits very well), and my family also needs me more than usual, I not only find my energy draining, but find it easier to ask, "Does any of this really need to be done right now?" Even if I have a list of items that maybe should be done before I go to bed, it is sometimes easier to just go to bed. That is clearly more characteristic of a Nine. It's not every day, and it's only at certain times, but it does show up as a reminder that I need to slow down. Some would call it a stress number response, and while at times that is true, I also know that there is something about type Nine characteristics I can choose when I know I need to slow down, to ponder, or reflect on a decision, rather than my typical rushed approach so that I can move on to another big task.

The other number I connect to across the arrows is Six. Six can represent characteristics I need to grow into, but that is also true for Nine. Both really represent opportunities for growth and transformation. I rarely slow down, to rest, which Nine can teach me, or to connect with others, which Six can teach me. The loyalist traits of a Six may be rooted in their anxious need for security, but they also remind us that Sixes are sometimes healthier feelers than thinkers. As a Three, I am more of a doer than a feeler. Nines are more thinkers than doers. Each of the numbers in this core triangle of the Enneagram have something to learn from the others. This is true for all of us.

My wife, an Eight, connects to Five and Two across her arrows. Like a Three, the Eight is a doer and is even more gut-centered and hands-on in their approach to life. Connecting to Five slows her body down and connects her to her head as a way to think through things before she acts. Connecting to Two helps her consider how others feel when she is on the go and otherwise reluctant to pause and feel.

To use the metaphor of colors again, if being a Three is red and a Nine is blue and a Six is yellow, then the shifts in my personality are reflected in the fact that my personality can shift from a violet tint to an orange one, but that at my core is red. I am always a Three, but the colors of these other numbers do shape me in meaningful ways.

Table 3.1 includes the nine core types and the numbers you can access most readily as a resource for your own growth. The next section provides more detail on how these other types relate to our core Enneagram type.

Table 3.1 Enneagram type connections.

Core Type	Triad	Wing	Wing	Arrow	Arrow
Two	Heart	One	Three	Four	Eight
Three	Heart	Two	Four	Six	Nine
Four	Heart	Three	Five	One	Two
Five	Head	Four	Six	Eight	Seven
Six	Head	Five	Seven	Nine	Three
Seven	Head	Six	Eight	Five	One
Eight	Hand	Seven	Nine	Two	Five
Nine	Hand	Eight	One	Three	Six
One	Hand	Nine	Two	Seven	Four

ENNEAGRAM LEVELS OF HEALTH

The Enneagram presents a more dynamic understanding of personality than most personality-related tools resources. The four dimensions of Myers-Briggs, as one common example, are pretty static. The top five strengths associated with CliftonStrengths (formerly Clifton StrengthsFinder), another tool that organizations often use, are not in flux. And while it is true that with the Enneagram you have one core number that doesn't change, your personality is different in different situations. The arrows and wings help us understand these shifts.

At the same time, another characteristic of the Enneagram that helps explain how we function differently in different situations is what Riso and Hudson call our levels of development. They propose nine levels of development for each of the nine types. The nine levels fall in three ranges: a healthy range, an average range, and an unhealthy range (Riso and Hudson, 1999).

According to Riso and Hudson, most of us spend most of our lives in the average range. Here, we live with the imbalance of our three dimensions. Here is where we tend to be driven to pursue the core desire of our type and try to meet the basic need. Here, the passion of our number drives us. Here, we live out some of the strengths of our number, but tend to overfocus on them, assuming they are what makes us who we are. Instead, it is in this average range where the best of who we are becomes the worst of who we are. In this average, unconscious way that we live out our personality with a lack of self-awareness, on autopilot as

Gurdjieff describes, we overrely on these distinct strengths of our number much like the carpenter whose only tool is a hammer treats everything as if it were a nail.

Riso and Hudson (1999) say that in average space we are not only less aware of how our personality is driving us, but we are also more identified with our negative ego patterns. The habitual, automatic responses of our personality reflect less conscious functions and less freedom in our responses, and at the same time, more compulsive and self-defeating ways of behaving.

If this is how we function in average levels, we must realize that we can always move further down the levels to the truly unhealthy levels. Here, we are at our most compulsive and reactive levels of functioning, or dysfunction. We can be truly destructive, and for each number the risks associated with less and less mental health are seen here.

In the other direction, we can also move up the levels to healthy functioning. We can pause, take a few deep breaths, and find ourselves in a healthier position.

Just in talking about these levels, we see times and situations where these things are true. We are tempted to focus more energy on these positive traits. Just the attention given to reading and reflecting on this does create in us some healthy reflexivity and awareness. We are more awake and present as we think about who we are and who we long to be. This is part of the value of self-awareness: just taking time to be mindful does help us function in a more healthy way. At the same time, seeing and naming just how healthy we think we are allows the ego to step in and remind us of why we want to be healthy, why we like to think of ourselves as healthy. Like the "Chutes and Ladders" game come to life, we constantly move up and down our levels of health. Just saying "look how healthy I am" can in and of itself be a slide down the psychological chute to the average functioning of our personality; on the other hand, an honest assessment of "look how difficult this is for me to navigate knowing my personality gets in the way" is a healthy invitation to take a few steps up the ladder.

We really are in a constant movement up and down these levels. Up the ladder in moments of awareness and intuition, and down the chute when we focus too much on how well we think we are doing, or on how far we think we have come. Not only are we moving vertically up and down, but as we make these moves, we simultaneously move across the Enneagram along the arrow lines and back and forth to our wings. We often think of the Enneagram as a two-dimensional image on a flat surface, but if we can imagine that the Enneagram has depth as well, then we can imagine a three-dimensional image of the Enneagram shape. One that captures more accurately the ups and downs of life that are reflective of our personality.

In light of this, we can revisit Escher's work and truly see how we are moving up one moment, turn a corner, and be moving in a downward direction. What does this mean practically for our numbers? As a Three, I mentioned my movement to Six and Nine. I described how the Nine part of my personality shows up at the end of a long day when I am ready to crash, but can also be something I engage in the middle of the day when I realize I need to slow down, take a break, and ponder and reflect rather than pushing through one decision after another.

When I add my levels of health to this description, I recognize how my automatic pilot version of myself is focused on achieving goals to prove my worth, is worried about how I compare to others and how I am perceived. I find myself taking on projects, saying yes to things that should not be on my to-do list because it seems like the nice thing to do, and because there is some value I am demonstrating when I say yes and when I prove just how much I can accomplish.

Sounds exhausting, right? So, it is easy to shift from this average or unhealthy way of functioning as a Three into unhealthy characteristics of a Nine. Down the chute I go in my own unhealthy path and over to equally unhealthy patterns in a number that is a resource for me, that can help me achieve balance. But when I slide down the chute into Nine, this resource point leads me to check out, or space out, by becoming disengaged and inattentive. I become impatient and stubborn, and going to bed always seems like the easiest solution.

While this is a more automatic, habitual response, I do have the choice to recognize when I am not in a healthy space as a Three. I can see my fear of being worthless, my need to be admired, and my desire to feel valuable. If I wake up to how I am functioning in these moments, rather than sliding down into less healthy Three behaviors and then unhealthy Nine behaviors, I can choose to use the resource that this arrow number is for me and I can engage in some healthy Nine responses.

I can take a deep breath, work with others for the sake of shared goals, and not strive to prove my own worth. I can seek harmony, use some mediation skills to allow me to be patient, serene, and content with how things are going and to see the value in working with others. In this, my inner drive to be a doer helps me to stop and think, and at the same time to engage my feelings. It might not last more than the duration of a single meeting before my ego kicks back in and I am climbing the ladder or falling back down another chute, but the more mindful I am of this pattern and my ability to make choices about my responses rather than being stuck in autopilot, the more healthy and balanced I can be as a leader.

To help us see this range of options for each of the numbers, I present the following chart for each number that includes the need of each number and a snapshot of what you can draw from the unhealthy as well as healthy elements of the numbers to which our core number connects. I also provide an image of each number with these connections to other numbers shown. Remember, my approach is less about which arrow is related to stress or security, to integration or disintegration, as some teach, and more about each of the numbers as resources from which you draw given the dynamic nature and the need that shape our personality.

ONES and their connections (see Figure 3.1)

ONES	**Need**	You have a need to be right, to be a person of integrity. On average, your need drives you to be idealistic and focused on how things should be. Below average, in less healthy times, your drive for perfection can be self-righteous, intolerant, and judgmental. Above average, you value what is right and accept other views to guide your actions.
	One → Seven	Ones can draw from Sevens an unhealthy tendency to be indulgent by giving into escapism, but they can also learn the freedom of adventure, a willingness to be lighthearted, and the value of positive connections with less focus on control.
	One → Four	Ones can draw from Fours an unhealthy temptation to withdraw in moody lament, or a healthy connection to their true inner feelings and an acceptance of their emotions.

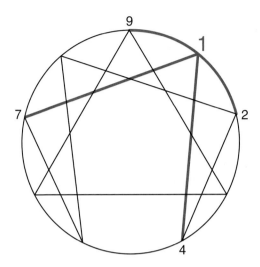

FIGURE 3.1

TWOS and their connections (see Figure 3.2)

TWOS	**Need**	You need to be needed and appreciated. On average, you are loving and giving, but good intentions drive you to assume you know how to care best. You need others to see your care. Below average, you believe you are indispensable, can be overbearing and your help is manipulative and self-serving. Above average, your humility allows you to see good in others and value in yourself.
	Two → Four	Twos can draw from Fours a depth of feeling that can become an unhealthy neediness and overreliance on others, but also a healthy focus on your own feelings and an inner depth when you connect to your own needs.
	Two → Eight	Twos can draw from Eights an unhealthy desire to be angry and controlling, or a healthy ability to set boundaries and express your true needs.

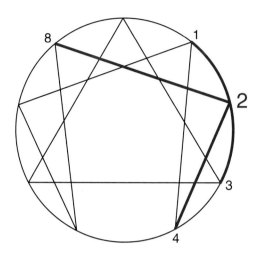

FIGURE 3.2

THREES and their connections (see Figure 3.3)

THREES	**Need**	You need to feel valued and successful. On average, you are driven to achieve and present an image of being successful. Below average, you fear failure and are deceptive in doing whatever it takes to look good and feel valued. Above average, you are authentic in being inner-directed and attuned to others.
	Three → Six	Threes can draw from Sixes an unhealthy anxiety and suspicion of others, or a healthy focus on others that allows you to share the attention you value.
	Three → Nine	Threes can draw from Nines an unhealthy apathy and desire to check out, or a healthy recognition that we don't have to drive ourselves to accomplishment at all times.

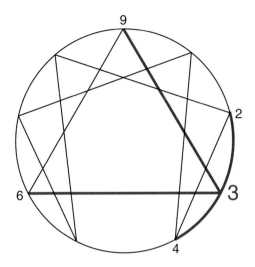

FIGURE 3.3

FOURS and their connections (see Figure 3.4)

FOURS	**Need**	You need to be seen as special or unique. On average, you are emotional in expressing yourself and protecting your self-image. You focus on fantasy and imagination by withdrawing. Below average, you focus on how different you are from others and misunderstood. You feel shame and torment pushing others away. Above average, you are self-aware and sensitive, creative in your endeavors.
	Four → One	Fours can draw from Ones an unhealthy criticism of their situation and a need to be right, or a healthy ability to focus on what is good and right as they focus on order and action.
	Four → Two	Fours can draw from Twos an unhealthy overreliance on connection and pulling people in, or a healthy outward focus on others and their needs and experiences.

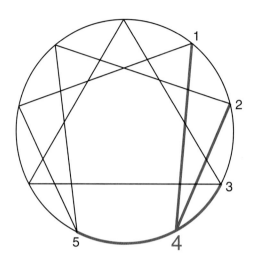

FIGURE 3.4

FIVES and their connections (see Figure 3.5)

FIVES	**Need**	You need to understand and be competent. On average, you want to understand before you act. You are detached as you seek your own way. Below average, you pull away from others and are cynical about connection, which takes energy from making sense of the world around you. Above average, you are innovative in your understanding of things, leading you to be open-minded and inventive.
	Five → Eight	Fives can draw from Eights an unhealthy cynicism and need to be in control, but also a healthy ability to assert themselves in being active and engaged in what needs to be done.
	Five → Seven	Fives can draw from Sevens an unhealthy and excessive drive for freedom, or a healthy outgoing focus on connecting with others.

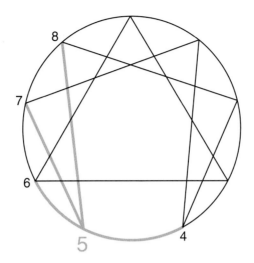

FIGURE 3.5

SIXES and their connections (see Figure 3.6)

SIXES	**Need**	You need to be safe and secure. On average, your caution and ambivalence send mixed signals. Though you desire connection and community, you question yourself and others. Below average, you feel fearful and inferior, insecure but seeking authority to address your fears. Above average, you have a responsible focus on others, can affirm yourself and others, and connect in meaningful ways that value cooperation.
	Six → Nine	Sixes can draw from Nines an unhealthy apathy and disengagement, and in a healthy way a grounded acceptance of life's circumstances.
	Six → Three	Sixes can draw from Threes an unhealthy need for shortcuts to get things done or a healthy and confident sense of drive and achievement in partnership with others.

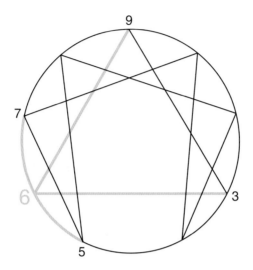

FIGURE 3.6

SEVENS and their connections (see Figure 3.7)

SEVENS	**Need**	You need to be free and to avoid pain. On average, you value your options and the adventures that are available to you. Below average, you feel uninhibited in taking on the world, impulsive, not knowing when to stop. Above average, you are lively and resilient, seeing the goodness of life and the true meaning of your actions.
	Seven → Five	Sevens can draw from Fives an unhealthy tendency to pull away and disengage, or a healthy critical reflection that leads to clear insight.
	Seven → One	Sevens can draw from Ones a resentful need to control others, or a healthy organized and practical focus on priorities.

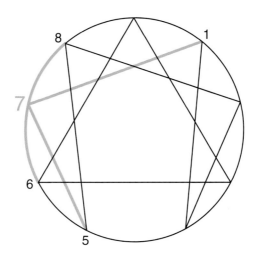

FIGURE 3.7

EIGHTS and their connections (see Figure 3.8)

EIGHTS	Need	You need to be in control. On average, your strength is your guide. You are decisive and commanding, passionate and assertive. Below average, you are controlling and combative if your vision is challenged. You over-extend yourself in your desire to get your way. Above average, your confident inner drive has restraint and self-control as you exhibit generosity with others' desires.
	Eight → Two	Eights can draw from Twos an unhealthy desire to control others when they think they know what is best, or a healthy practice of care and guidance for people who are vulnerable.
	Eight → Five	Eights can draw from Fives an unhealthy disconnection from others to be in their heads, or a healthy commitment to reflection and more strategic, thoughtful action.

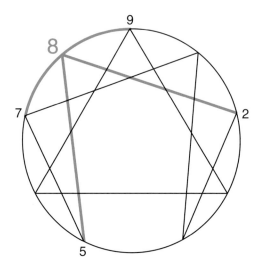

FIGURE 3.8

NINES and their connections (see Figure 3.9)

NINES	Need	You need to avoid conflict. On average, you are active, but in your own way, indifferent to others and you seek harmony through resignation. Below average, you are stubborn and disengaged. You feel incapable of facing challenges and minimize problems to keep the peace. Above average, you deeply sense your value. You are optimistic and reflective as you influence others for good.
	Nine → Three	Nines can draw from Threes an unhealthy merging, doing things just to get along, or a healthy focus on action and engagement helping them to be productive in meaningful ways.
	Nine → Six	Nines can draw from Sixes an unhealthy pondering that leaves them pessimistic and anxious, or a healthy concern for what needs to be done in life.

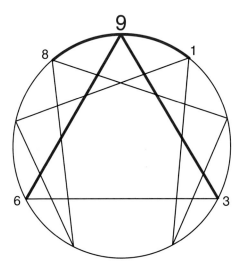

FIGURE 3.9

These connections are part of your path to transformation. What can you learn about the numbers to which you are connected in order to see elements within them that are true for you? Learning to see and understand your core type is essential in Enneagram work, but it is also helpful to see these connections and what these other numbers can teach you about your personality.

The Enneagram is a dynamic tool with a rich history and numerous layers of meaning. It can be so useful in so many ways if we take the time to explore its various dimensions. Most of us learn our number and then wonder what comes next. I hope this chapter gives you some depth of background in the dynamic nature of your personality. These building blocks help us begin to explore the heights of Enneagram wisdom. We have seen how the nine types are organized and how they can influence and help us develop a sense of balance. We explore this more in the next few chapters as we turn to Unit Two and the role of the three Enneagram dimensions.

UNIT TWO

Unit One introduced the Enneagram and the three dimensions of feeling, thinking, and doing that make you who you are as a leader. It also included other components of the Enneagram that can help you understand the structure and significance of this tool, resources that may help you begin to identify your type if you are not familiar with it already. In addition, it helped you understand the importance of the other numbers around the Enneagram that relate to your core type, your wings, and the numbers across the lines.

Learning to wake up to our sense of self, to practice self-observation, and to see how our personality works within us with dynamic potential for growth is the core of the Enneagram. This growth requires us to understand in more depth the role of feeling, thinking, and doing as three dimensions of personality, and of leadership. The Enneagram helps us learn to see these characteristics within ourselves and to balance the way they function in our lives.

We all have the capacity *to feel* in connection with others, *to think* through the relevant information available to us, and *to do* the work that is required of us as leaders. However, we are each driven by one of these three dimensions on the one hand, and on the other, one of these three dimensions requires some development. Ultimately, we must learn to see all three clearly as we strive to balance them on our journey to healthy leadership.

In Unit Two, we return to these three dimensions and the way that they function for each Enneagram personality type. While the goal is to balance our use of these dimensions in our approach to leadership, none of us does that very well. Each of us subconsciously prioritizes our approach to the three dimensions in a manner that is distinct to our type. As part of recognizing this, we will learn how the dimension that we prioritize most in our personality is called the dominant dimension of our personality. We will learn how a second, or support, dimension reinforces the dominant one. Then, we will learn what it means for each type to repress one of the three dimensions. This overall structure, with specific attention to the repressed dimension, will help us see a particular social stance that we take as leaders given our Enneagram type. This is the result of the three dimensions being out of balance.

After learning the implications of these stances, we turn to Unit Three to learn some practices we can develop to bring balance to our lives and the way we lead.

CHAPTER FOUR

THE DOMINANT DIMENSION RESULTING IN ENNEAGRAM TRIADS

Coronavirus took a toll on higher education as it did in every industry and in every aspect of our lives. In addition, the second pandemic of racial reckoning shook our nation in 2020 and pushed us all to consider the effects of race and racism in our lives. During our 2021 school year, my academic leadership team had to respond to both. We are not a large school, but as you might imagine, we had a wide range of reactions to these challenges. My leaders did extraordinary work, as did our entire faculty and staff. As social workers, we were explicit in our support for the health of our most vulnerable and the care of our most marginalized, but we still made mistakes. Despite our best efforts, we operate as part of larger systems that perpetuate some of the challenges. I have been willing to admit my own struggles in not always seeing what we needed and not always acting as quickly or thoroughly as needed.

On May 25, 2020, George Floyd was murdered under the knee of a police officer. A week later, our school released a statement offering our care and support for Black lives. To many of our students, we were silent for several days. Behind the scenes, there was not much silence. Immediately, I heard from a few of our leaders who were worried about the safety of our own students and who were wanting to make sure we were asking the right questions and getting the information we needed to communicate effectively when we did eventually release a statement. A few of our leaders wanted us to reach out and connect with colleagues and students of color to hear what they were going through and felt bad we had not done so already. And, a few of our leaders were pushing for a clear message to go out immediately and grew more frustrated with each passing day. A significant part of what I learned to see is just how differently we react to these crises.

Our own experiences of race and culture were a factor in our responses. Gender, age, and other elements of identity played a role as well. I also knew the personalities of our leaders were at play in how we each engaged the conversation and our planning that week. More than numbers, what I saw were the three triads of the Enneagram shaping our responses. The heart dominant leaders connected with their shame for letting people down, me included. The head dominant leaders engaged with anxiety and concern for what we knew and what we needed to know. The hand dominant leaders, angry for our slow reaction times, wanted more immediate action. They all had the support of our staff, faculty, and students at the center of everything they did that week and I knew I had to navigate a range of responses in my own role as our dean.

To help me understand our responses, I turned to the teachings of Father Thomas Keating. Keating was a Trappist Monk who was best known for his recent rediscovery of a contemplative approach to prayer in Christian life called centering prayer. As part of his spiritual practice workshops, he taught that humans are prone to engage in one of three programs that work unconsciously within us as we seek our own fulfillment in response to life's struggles. These programs represent a deep need that drives our actions unconsciously. We each operate out of a need for affection and approval, a need for security and survival, or a need for power and control (Keating 1999).

Keating did not make the Enneagram connection in his writings, but Father Richard Rohr helps connect the dots. Rohr (2013b) points out that heart triad types, with their shame core, are shaped by a need for affection and approval. Head triad types, with their experience of fear, have a need for security and survival. And hand triad types, rooted in anger, are driven by a need for power and control. In the following, we begin looking at the triads with a recognition of how heart, head, and hands are part of what motivates the behavior of each Enneagram type.

I can see Keating's three programs for happiness in my leadership team's responses to racism and other needs we are addressing in our community and culture. I see them in my family, in our different types and needs and what motivates us in our relationships. Do you see them in yourself? As you learn more about the triads and the extent to which either feeling, thinking, or doing is dominant in your personality, do you sense the influence this has in your life? The way it drives your personality? Motivates your behavior? As is often the case, we are asleep to these forces within us, but with this knowledge comes new awareness of how these characteristics are at work. Can you see them?

We will look at more details for each of the Enneagram types in this chapter, highlighting similarities within the triads based on the power of feeling, thinking, and doing as a dominant dimension that drives each of the nine Enneagram types.

THE ROLE OF THE DOMINANT DIMENSION

Triads represent the most common grouping of numbers within the Enneagram and they are based on which of the core dimensions drives, or is dominant in, a person's personality. Is your personality predominantly driven by heart-related feeling? Head-centered thinking? Hands-engaged doing?

Hurley and Donson call the dimension that dominates our personality our "preferred center" and describe how each of us prefers one of the three centers because we mistakenly think it provides certain advantages (Hurley and Dobson 1991). As a result of this preference, we unconsciously overuse our dominant center and it mechanically shapes our way of life. As examples, let us consider a Two, Five, and Eight. A Two values feelings but does not always see the ways that a desire for connection controls them. A Five realizes they are in their heads but may not see just how rarely they step away from a compelling need to understand their environment. An Eight knows they want to be in charge but may not see their intense need for control.

As a result of this, each type forgets how to balance our use of the other two dimensions and also fails to recognize how the dominant dimension best operates. This means that we each misuse our dominant dimension. Again, a Two assumes the value of others' feelings, but may not see the value of their own feelings. A Five, in their focus on observing and taking in information, may not know when or how to share or apply the knowledge they have collected in a meaningful way. And an Eight, believing they are doing what needs to be done, may not be able to understand how to trust someone else's approach to their work. It is as though this one dimension that drives our personality is the hammer of our personality's toolbox and all of life's needs and struggles are like a nail.

Not only do we misuse our dominant dimension, but we fail to allow the other two dimensions to function at their full level. This dimension of our personality over-operates or extends itself beyond the appropriate bounds of its function. A Two will try to solve a challenging intellectual problem relationally. A Five wants to slow down and understand a scenario when it requires their immediate action. An Eight can work in such a way that prevents them from listening to a trusted friend when that is what is most needed.

In order to understand how these automatic preferences shape us, consider if a feeling-based response would be preferred when trying to make sure our taxes are filed correctly. Probably not, so a Two may have to move beyond their automatic way of feeling in order to accomplish this task that is not heart-centered. Is a preference for thinking what we need when a big project is due by the end of the day? The time for thinking may have passed and what a type Five may need in that moment is the ability to focus on doing. Is the drive of a doing dominant type what we need most when sitting with a grieving friend? An Eight may disagree, but doing something about grief in this situation might not be as helpful as being open to feelings of pain and loss.

Hurley and Donson help us make sense of this by describing how our dominant dimension is what we use to take in information over and over again throughout the course of a day. This dimension is both a lens and a blinder, they say. "As a lens, it focuses our attention" (Hurley and

Donson 2000). However, because the lens is so dominant in our life, it strains our vision and distorts the image that we are trying to focus on. When a Four automatically responds to a crisis by feeling instead of doing, their view can be out of focus. When a Five wants to think through a situation that requires a feeling response, their experience can be blurred. The lens of our personality type provides a faulty, but ever present, way of seeing the world around us.

Likewise, as a blinder, the dominant dimension prevents us from using the other two centers. A Four habitually responds with feeling, and how to engage doing or thinking is often blocked from sight. The head response of a Five focuses on a mechanical thinking-through of a situation, blinding them to the use of their heart or hands. The lens of our personality blurs our vision and the blinder of our personality limits our use of the three dimensions that work within us.

A part of the curse of coronavirus for me was moving from the use of reading glasses on occasion to wearing all-day progressive lenses. Progressives are a step beyond bifocals in that their lenses have three levels of *vision adjustment*. These glasses bring balance to my sight. They help me use the level of *correction* appropriate to the item I am trying to see. My uncorrected eyesight right now functions much like my personality. Without my glasses, I see distance really well, but not all of life is at a distance. I hold my phone out as far as my long arms will allow, but it is still not enough for my bad eyes. Using my distant sight for close-up items just doesn't work. I need an adjustment to see the things that are closest to me.

Likewise, using one of three dimensions of our personality to respond to all of life's opportunities and demands does not serve us well. It provides a limited and blurry approach to leadership, and whether we see it or not, this is what drives us. Let us now turn to the three Enneagram triads to see which dimension is dominant for each Enneagram type, what it means for that dimension to be dominant in our personality, and how it gets corrupted when unintentionally but universally overused. As part of this, we will see a core emotional response associated with each triad and learn how shame, fear, and anger shape our personality.

Heart Triad

The heart triad types of Two, Three, and Four are feeling dominant (see Figure 4.1), which is to say that feelings are the most dominant of the

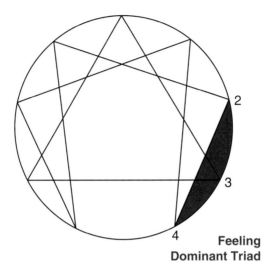

**Feeling
Dominant Triad**

FIGURE 4.1 Feeling dominant triad.

three core dimensions motivating these personality types. Feelings shape this triad more than they realize. People who identify with one of these Enneagram types are relationship-focused. They are often in touch with the nature of feelings and how important they are to human relationships. At the same time, they can be so heart-centered that their feelings overwhelm them. These types are feeling dominant, but being dominated by feelings is not always ideal.

The nature of the heart dimension of the human soul is to shape our understanding of identity. The qualities of the heart are the source of identity for all of us, and not just the heart triad. In fact other numbers may have a healthier sense of identity influenced by their heart dimension used in a balanced way. In part, this is because this triad is so relationship focused that they struggle to find a clear sense of self.

The desire for relationships is important to most people, but for this group it is essential. These numbers value connection more than the other triads. They want to engage in relationship for the sake of genuine heart-felt care for others, but there is a need to be appreciated, valued, and seen that motivates the heart triad. They want others to pay attention, to notice them, and to appreciate what they bring to a relationship.

This approach to feelings influences the relational needs of these numbers, forces them to lose their sense of identity, and leads them to be image-focused and overly self-conscious in their desire to win over people. These three types worry about how people perceive them and long for the approval of others. Shame is a common response when you long for connection and meaningful relationships at every turn, particularly when relationships are challenging. When our experiences in relationships don't live up to our high expectations, shame is a core emotion that heart-driven people carry within themselves.

Many people who identify with a heart type would say feelings are central, maybe even that feelings are all that really matter. However, because the dominant dimension often functions in a way that is not obvious to us, in a subconscious manner, feelings tend to control these types, rather than them being in control of their feelings.

These types respond to the people and situations around them day in and day out from a heart perspective and are not even aware of it. This often means that these types are not necessarily the best feelers—they may not be the most in touch with their feelings and they may not have the healthiest emotional responses. They are driven by their feelings, but they might not even recognize the full extent to which their focus on relationships influences them on a daily basis.

One of the ways to know your number is to look beyond the behaviors associated with each type and to focus on the underlying motivation. Twos are often named Helpers or Givers. Helping is a behavior that is true for many people who are not Twos. And valuing relationships and being helpful is something Sixes see in themselves that make them wonder whether they may be a Two or a Six. The motivations behind the helping is more important for identifying your number than the behaviors we may associate with that type.

What are the factors that comprise the motivation for each number? Riso and Hudson teach that each number has a "basic fear." We can each experience the fears of the other numbers; however, the core fear of our number shapes us most deeply, even if unconsciously. They write that our fear "terrorizes us so completely that we have to defend ourselves against it in order to function" (Riso and Hudson 1999).

Adding to the negative motivation of fear, Riso and Hudson (1999) provide a positive motivating factor, a "basic desire" that exists for each type. Similar to the basic fear, this unconscious desire is a deep motivating factor. Rohr adds another layer to how we understand what unconsciously motivates the core of our personality by talking about the core need of each number (Rohr and Ebert 2001). As you read through these motivations for each number, do you have awareness of your underlying fear, desire, or need? Can you bring to consciousness what the deep motivation is for the way your personality functions without you knowing it?

Two: What motivates a Two? Why are Twos motivated in such a way that they are labeled as Helpers? Helping, and the desire for a nurturing relationship, is rooted in their basic fear, desire, and need. The basic fear of a Two is of being unworthy of being loved and it follows that their desire is to be loved. They have a need to be needed and appreciated. Shame plays a role in this; it can be said that shame motivates a Two, and it does to the extent that they focus their shame outwardly. Their need to be needed plays out in an intense focus on others. Twos are primarily focused on the feelings of others rather than focusing on their own. A close friend who is a Two not only sees herself as a Two because she is helpful or giving, though she truly is; she knows she is a Two when she catches herself focused on others and meeting their needs in an effort to please them or connect with them. She can then take an honest look at herself recognizing her unconscious fear of not being appreciated, needed, or loved.

Three: Threes are also motivated by connection, but less on a personal and relational level. They have a fear of being worthless or without value. The desire of a Three is to be valuable and worthwhile in the eyes of everyone around them. They have a deep need to have value or to succeed. More importantly, perhaps, they have a need to avoid failure. The need for being valued is so deep, and they are so blind to it that they are often out of touch with feeling shame. Threes avoid shame like they avoid most feelings. As a Three, when I am honest with myself, and not pretending otherwise, I want everyone around me to see what I am worth, and anything that results in shame is hidden far out of sight. I will stay on the move, hustling for love, doing whatever it takes to prove my value.

Four: Fear of being without identity or personal significance is what motivates a Four. The desire of Fours is to be uniquely oneself. They have a need to be authentic. As such, Fours are much more in touch with their sense of shame. They focus their shame inwardly, with an intense reflective posture on the nature of what they are feeling. A Four I know and love has a deep longing to be seen, to be really seen, to be known for who he is. He has several behaviors we associate with a Four; he is creative and loves music, but he is absolutely aware of what shame feels like. He feels his feelings deeply in an unconscious drive to find and express his true self.

Curt Thompson, author of *The Soul of Shame,* writes that we feel guilt for what we have done and we feel shame for who we are (Thompson 2015). To this, Brene Brown describes shame as a "painful feeling or experience of believing we are flawed and therefore unworthy of love and belonging—something we've experienced, done, or failed to do makes us unworthy of connection" (Brown 2012).

For leaders in the heart triad, how we see ourselves matters and too often we see shame for who we are. Relationships matter, and the thought of being unworthy of connection is a place of great pain, whether or not we think of it as shame. We want our staff, faculty, and students to see our value, to love us, and to see our significance. As a result, Twos, Threes, and Fours are in the heart triad; we are feeling dominant, and we carry with us a sense of shame, as shown in Figure 4.2.

Feeling dominant types can recognize this and learn to see ourselves and the teams for whom we are responsible in a new light. We can learn to recognize the need for affection and approval that drives us. We can

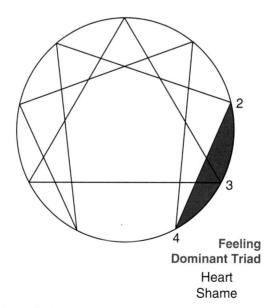

2

3

4

**Feeling
Dominant Triad**

Heart
Shame

FIGURE 4.2 Heart triad.

open our heart in new ways to see our value from within. Our identity is not in how others see us, it is not in how we want to be seen; the truest qualities of our heart are the source of our identity. We can be honest about how we feel and we can more genuinely connect to others.

We may know that we are loved and loveable, but it is not easy to let that conscious message seep into the places where our unconscious doubts motivate our daily behavior and the ways we look for love. Twos, Threes, and Fours, you are deeply loved, at all times, just as you are.

Head Triad

If this heart-oriented language is not at the core of what motivates the habitual patterns of your personality, maybe you are in the thinking triad driven by the functions of your head. Thinking is what is most dominant in the way personality functions for types Five, Six, and Seven (see Figure 4.3). Similar to how the feeling triad sees the heart at work within them, thinking types may recognize that they are more in their heads on a daily basis, and that logic and a clear rationale should drive our approach to life. However, because thinking is also often unconsciously driving these types, they may not be aware of how in their heads they are on a daily basis. Not being able to get out of their heads may be a way of

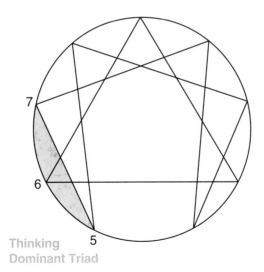

FIGURE 4.3 Thinking dominant triad.

recognizing how thinking controls them, rather than them being able to control what is happening in their heads. Overthinking their way through life is a common experience for these types.

While relationships are at the core of functioning for the heart triad, for the head triad, it is a focus on safety, security, and a strategy to assure these things. Leaders in this triad value information more than the other triads. They do want information for the sake of knowledge, but there is a need to know in order to feel safe and secure in the world.

Being head dominant also means these leaders value data and research. They focus on compiling information, analyzing it, and using it to inform their decision-making. This is a logical and rational focus, and it is a focus they assume everyone has. These three types worry about having the information they need in order to feel competent, to feel safe, to avoid feeling pain. When ideas and information are at the forefront of your mind, and your mind is at the forefront of what guides you, you will realize that you cannot know everything you desire to know, and fear is a common experience. When you are afraid you don't know enough to feel secure, and when you realize you can never know enough, anxiety is a core emotion and it is one that shapes the experience of the head triad types.

Five: Fear and a longing for security function as motivating factors for the thinking types. The motivation of a Five is a fear of being incapable or incompetent. They are aware of their head knowledge, but they do have a desire to be useful. They have a need to understand. You can see how fear can be a part of this motivating drive for a Five. Fives are comfortable with what they know and how to take information in, but the world is overwhelming and frightening, and so their fear is focused outwardly; knowing how to function in the world is fearful for Fives.

Six: For a Six, their core fear is of being without support or guidance in the world. They have a desire to be secure and a deep need to be safe. There is never a guarantee that we will be safe and secure, and so Sixes just live in the world this way. They focus their fear inwardly, afraid to trust themselves and also focus their fear outwardly, afraid of the world around them. If they cannot trust themselves, how can they trust others? This fear may be too much and so they avoid their fear; this may mean they are out of touch with just how fearful they are, of just how anxious they are in their way of being in the world.

Just as Threes are out of touch with both shame and much of their feeling center, Sixes may know they are afraid, but may not see how living in fear shapes the questions they are always asking and their struggle to be confident in their thinking center. Whereas for Threes, the desire to be valued by others is a truncated approach to feelings, with Sixes, the need to ask questions is a truncated approach to thinking. It may feel like it supports thinking, but in reality it inhibits the development of a clear and quiet mind.

Seven: Sevens are known for their adventurous spirit, and while the world around them is not as frightening to them, they do have a deep fear of being trapped in pain. The desire of the Seven is to be happy and they have a need to be cheerful. Sevens want to be free, they want a world without limitations, and the most frightening thing they face is the world within themselves, so their fear is focused inwardly. The interior world of grief and sadness is where they experience fear and what they are seeking to avoid. Sevens can think about these feelings, and about how to solve them, but sitting with the feelings is the most difficult experience for a Seven. "Surely there is something I can do to help" said a Seven who thought he was a Two because he wanted to help people fix what they were feeling. The Twos in the room knew better; they could see the difference in their ability to sit with feelings. Avoiding the pain rather than sitting with the feelings is a realization this friend made in learning to identify as a Seven.

In one of his most famous speeches, Nelson Mandela said, "I learned that courage was not the absence of fear, but the triumph over it. The brave man is not he who does not feel afraid, but he who conquers that fear" (Mandela 1995). Likewise, Glennon Doyle, author of *Love Warrior*, writes, "Courage is the presence of fear, and going anyway" (Doyle 2016). Whether that fear is of the world around you, as is often the case for a Five, or of the world within you, for a Seven, courage is the antidote to fear. For Fives, Sixes, and Sevens, the thinking dominant orientation, being in the head triad, also results in this group operating as the fear triad, as shown in Figure 4.4. You can experience fear and at the same time muster the courage to lead in effective ways. Leaders in the head triad are seeking knowledge as a way to inspire bravery; they must realize that faith is what inspires the courage needed to overcome our fears.

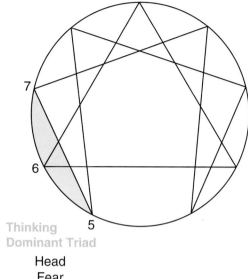

Thinking
Dominant Triad
Head
Fear

FIGURE 4.4 Head triad.

Head-oriented leaders can acknowledge this need for faith and courage. We will always be faced with big decisions where we just don't know enough and with deep pain that feels like it may pull us under. And, we can learn to lead with a sense of trust that despite our fear, our uncertainty, and our questioning of whether we know enough, our brave responses have great value to the teams that rely on us. Fives, Sixes, and Sevens, you can face your fear with courage, just as you are.

Hand Triad

Finally, the hand triad includes the types who trust their gut, who are active and engaged as doing-dominant personalities, the Eights, Nines, and Ones (see Figure 4.5). These types are known for their instinctive, even visceral, body presence, although they may be unaware of how active they are in the world. As hands-on kinds of people, their body drives them more than their head or their heart; they may wrestle with how to slow down. They may also be able to describe how and where they carry stress in their bodies more easily than other types.

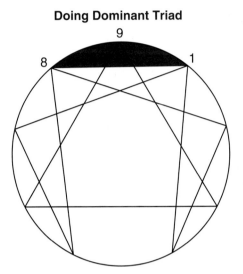

FIGURE 4.5 Doing dominant triad.

The desire to be in control is something many of us value; however, this group has a more intense instinctive drive to be in control of their response to life's situations. As we will see, the Nine's response may be slower and more even keeled and the Eight and One more driven and engaged, but they each want to do things the way they feel is best. Autonomy and freedom are important to how they function in the world.

Because these types value control and want to do things their way, when things go wrong or they are not able to be in control of their response, the common response in this triad is anger. While their anger is not always direct, and may be expressed as frustration or disappointment, there is an annoyance or exasperation that we experience with these types when they are not able to exert their desire in or be in control of a situation.

Eight: What factors are unconsciously motivating these doing dominant types? For an Eight, it is the fear of being controlled or harmed by others. It makes sense then that the desire of the Eight is to protect oneself and that they need to be in control, or at least not controlled, in any situation. The anger of the hand triad is most obvious in an Eight. They are comfortable with conflict and do not see expressing anger as a problem. Their anger is externally focused, not necessarily on others, but expressed outwardly. A student who identified as an Eight said that she preferred to think of herself as "conflict forward"—a very kind way to describe an emotion that is difficult for the rest of us and second nature to an Eight. The common misconception with people who are this comfortable with anger is that they are controlling; hence, the label "bossy." What is truer for an Eight is their unconscious need to be not controlled by others. It is a concern about being controlled that can result in the expressive anger we associate with Eights.

Nine: The Fear of loss of connection, or fragmentation, is what motivates a Nine. This is coupled with a desire to be at peace. The Nine has a need to avoid conflict. While the Eight is conflict forward, a Nine is more often conflict avoidant. It is conflict, they believe, that brings about disconnection. Avoiding conflict, they hope, can be a way to avoid anger. However, they must learn to see that trying to avoid conflict is oftentimes what leads to conflict. And, while Nines are trying to avoid conflict, conflict has a way of finding each of us, and so their anger is more likely to be passive aggressive. A dear friend of ours was so fearful our children would not get along that she would pack up and leave without saying goodbye in order to avoid potential conflict. We would look up and notice she was gone; later she would describe something her daughter had done that made her think a fight was coming.

One: The fear of type Ones is being bad, or evil, or corrupt. Their desire to be a person of integrity, whose actions and way of being in the world is good and right. They have the need to be right, to do what is right. Some describe it as a need to be perfect; however, most Ones do not see themselves as able to be perfect and dismiss the common One label of "perfectionist." The anger of the Ones is expressed internally, usually in terms of a frustration with themselves or a critical lens focused inward. It is expressed quietly and with principled self-control, largely because being angry is not something a good person does, so they find it difficult to own their anger. A long-time friend moved and for years it was difficult to keep the relationship strong. She apologized for letting me down when we both knew I was the one who was slow to return calls. I could tell that while she was upset with me, she would not say it and was even more angry with herself for not making the relationship work better at the time.

Thich Nhat Hanh has a book entitled *Anger* with a subtitle: *Wisdom for Cooling the Flames*. In it, he writes, "Hope is important because it can make the present moment less difficult to bear" (Hanh 2002). He goes on to talk about the need to embrace our pain and tend to the difficult moments of life.

Controlling anger is not the answer, and the hand triad does value control. It is a desire to control and an inability to be in control that often creates our anger. Frustration, disappointment, and outright anger all result from the doing dimension driving our personality. With anger just under the surface for these three Enneagram types, this is known as the doing triad, hand triad, or anger triad (see Figure 4.6).

Trusting that change is possible is difficult for leaders in this triad who are often visceral in their response. Trust does not come easy when our automatic response is a desire for power and control. And yet, anger and frustration do not have to dominate the experiences of Eights, Nines, and Ones; these leaders can develop an openness to leading in new ways even while wanting to hold on to a sense of control—as long as we do not grip too tightly. As a result, you can have hope and patience just as you are.

The dominant center truly dominates our personality. Some of us are clearly more feeling than thinking in how we approach a situation. Some

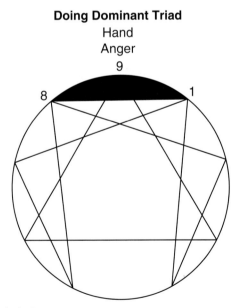

FIGURE 4.6 Hand triad.

prefer to trust our gut, a symbol of being doing dominant. And some of us are clearly thinkers first and foremost. The shame, fear, and anger that are just under the surface can also help us see how the dominant dimension drives our personality. We do not control these automatic emotional responses nearly as much as they control us. We do not choose to have a heart-first, head-first, or hand-first response, much less the fact that this response is mechanical and less than healthy. To be mechanical suggests that the way we lead is robotic, and in some ways it is. It is automatic in its functions and habitually exerts itself in the work of our personality. It often overfunctions and seldom functions according to the true purpose of the dimension. The result is that all three dimensions are out of balance in our personality. The dominant dimension triads are shown all together in Figure 4.7.

As one of my students who is a Two recently shared, "I don't want to throw my heart center out of the car; I just don't always want it to always be in the driver's seat." As she humbly recognized, the feeling

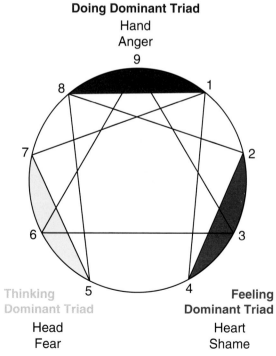

FIGURE 4.7 Enneagram dominant dimension triads.

dominant types do not necessarily offer the healthiest emotional response; they just connect at an emotional level first. The thinking dominant types are not always the smartest, but they do require everything to go through their head. And, being doing dominant does not mean you are the most productive, but that you always have a gut level, hands-on response.

For each of us, our dominant center does not provide our best response; it is just the first on the scene and is ready to go. As we will soon learn, there is a second dimension of our personality close behind ready to help reinforce this first one. The work for us is first to learn to see how this works. Then, we can reorient and repurpose these dimensions in a more balanced way while also engaging the third dimension that lags behind.

Again, the dominant center does not always function at its best, but it always functions first. And this is true day in and day out. It is true in our biggest decisions, the most stressful situations we face, and in daily matters that are far less urgent. It shows up in the good and the bad opportunities that face our schools and organizations.

A leader in my school who is a Two recently shared some reflections on how her personality showed up as she was developing mentoring relationships with new colleagues and in the stress of speaking to a large room where personal connections could not happen naturally. Another leader who is an Eight was recognizing the intensity she brings to her leadership from the daily tasks of preparing for class to the big challenge she took on to assure a living wage was paid to our graduate assistants. A Six who knows she wrestles to feel secure in her work asks a lot of questions about a simple matter that she has faced dozens of times and asked just as many on a much larger funding challenge facing her school.

Learning to wake up to the ways this dominant dimension shapes us is essential Enneagram work as we seek to lead in more effective ways. We may see how one dimension drives our personality, but even then we are not always convinced it is problematic. Can you see the dominant dimension driving your personality? Can you see how it shows up day in and day out? Is it more clear to you how balance of all three might be beneficial? Before we learn to release the power of this dominant dimension, we need more clarity on how the second and third are also

Table 4.1 Enneagram triads.

Type	Dominant Dimension	Triad
Two	Feeling	Heart
Three	Feeling	Heart
Four	Feeling	Heart
Five	Thinking	Head
Six	Thinking	Head
Seven	Thinking	Head
Eight	Doing	Hand
Nine	Doing	Hand
One	Doing	Hand

at work within us. In the next chapter, we turn to the role the second dimension plays in our personality.

This chapter identified the dominant dimension and triad for each of the nine Enneagram types. A reminder of this is provided in Table 4.1.

CHAPTER FIVE

THE SUPPORT DIMENSION RESULTING IN TWO DIMENSIONS DOING THE WORK OF THREE

We have begun to see how for each Enneagram type a dominant dimension of our personality drives the way we respond to everyday leadership situations. All three dimensions are needed; however, we live with them out of balance. The result is that one dimension is dominant and a second reinforces the dominant one; the third dimension lags far behind. Two dimensions do the work of three. Here are some examples of what this looks like.

Crystal is a colleague and academic leader in my school. She is passionate about creating an environment of equity and inclusion, and as a Latina leader, she always has ideas about what can be improved in our predominantly white institution. Ideas we need! She knows that, as a Seven, she is a thinking dominant type. She also knows that she has a lot of energy that is focused on launching her big ideas. Follow-through takes a little more work, but she loves innovation.

Nothing exemplified the thinking-then-doing approach as much as when Crystal spent the first year of her new enrollment management role completely overhauling our admissions process. She thoughtfully created a plan to improve the student experience from top to bottom, with equity and inclusion as a primary focus. Her thinking-minded approach helped build a solid foundation to launch a new program that continues this inclusive approach and helps set up students for success before they begin their classes.

In Crystal's leadership, we see an example of how the first two dimensions are stacked as they are subconsciously prioritized in our personality. Thinking, then doing, in her case. Crystal might not say that it is a conscious decision to think and then act in response to what she is thinking, but it is certainly her natural response to taking on a challenge as she leads.

"I think we ought to try" is the mindset of a Seven and something Crystal sees at work within herself. She describes it this way, "I will always say yes first when someone has a new idea because I don't ever want to be complacent and think the way we are doing things is the best way. We think about how to make an idea work and only when it doesn't fit our mission do we let it go."

Michael is a doctoral student and music minister on staff in a local church. He is creative and passionate about the ways music influences and inspires us. He sees the power for connection that comes from his work. Music clearly flows from the heart center and Michael feels that power. He knows he is a Four and he wants to use the power of his feeling orientation to nurture relationships. He approaches all aspects of life from this relational perspective, but then he finds himself dwelling on the options available to him. He stops to think through all the relationship scenarios, the good and the bad, the best and the worst. For his personality, we see the stacking of feeling then thinking.

In talking about relationships recently, Michael described this desire to connect as a heart-centered driver, and then he thinks about options related to making the relationships work or not work. He said he will feel and think and feel and think before eventually putting something into action for the sake of a relationship. Michael said that, as a Four, his heart is his center of gravity, like a centripetal force in a spiral that requires action to break the cycle. He values and needs this feeling orientation to be true to himself, but sometimes needs a way to break out of it.

With an understanding of how one of the three dimensions dominates our personality, we are now adding another layer to how these characteristics are stacked within us. The dominant dimension is what we automatically use to take in information, or to receive it. However, as soon as we take in information, we give it meaning and respond to what we take in. We each have a dominant dimension that receives and a secondary dimension that responds to what we receive.

THE RESPONSIVE ROLE OF THE SUPPORT DIMENSION

Maurice Nicoll was the student of Gurdjieff who made clear the pattern of how different personalities stack, or prioritize, feeling, thinking, and doing in different ways. Hurley and Donson found this work of Nicoll and expanded it. Nicoll said that this was an ordering of these dimensions within us and that we do not get to choose, or change, how they are oriented. In other words, it is the subconscious way these three dimensions are structured within us that creates the structure of the Enneagram types.

Hurley and Dobson (1991) call the first two dimensions at work within us the preferred center and the support center. Whatever life brings our way, we receive the situation and respond to it from two of the Enneagram dimensions. And, we each do this automatically with the same two dimensions over and over again.

In other words, as soon as we take in information, or receive it, we respond to it. Both of these functions are habitual and mechanical in our personality. We each do this using the combination of our primary and secondary dimension, or preferred and support centers. In our healthier moments, we can be present to ourselves and our situation and use the dimension that is needed for the task rather than the automatic response of the two dimensions that drive our personality. However, the personality response of our Enneagram type is driven by these two dimensions.

In a recent leadership workshop, I was asked if by "support center" I mean the center that helps the dominant center function in a more healthy way. While this can be true, it is usually the case that the support center's response reinforces the habitual patterns of the dominant center. It supports the dominant center in a less than healthy way.

In fact, Hurley and Donson describe how the preferred and support center work together in such an intertwined way that corrupts our personality. This leaves out the third of these dimensions, causing it to function as a repressed center. I will say more about the repressed center later. Here, it is important to remember their words, "The first two centers are doing the work of all three" (Hurley and Donson 2000). This is what causes imbalance in our lives and creates the structure of our personality. The support center props up and reinforces the dominant center all the while convincing us the third center is not important in our personality.

I seldom use the one-word names to describe the Enneagram types. The names are oversimplified characterizations, or generalizations, of much more complex personality patterns. One thing we can see in the names, however, is that many of them do help clarify the connection between the dominant and support center. For each type, I will describe how the names we sometimes hear reflect the role of these first two dimensions and how they interact in our personality.

To help us see how these two dimensions work, how the support center relates to the preferred center, for each of the nine types we make our way around the Enneagram and highlight each number. Figure 5.1 presents the prioritized stacking of the dominant and support dimensions for each Enneagram type, and I discuss these combinations for each type starting with the heart types and the Two. As we have seen, the middle type of the triad is unusual, so I will discuss each end before returning to the Three, Six, and Nine.

Twos. Twos are a feeling dominant type with a doing support center. They are in the feeling triad, but neighbor the doing triad. Their initial response is to feel and then to do something based on that feeling. This is what makes Twos commonly described as helpers. The feeling dimension

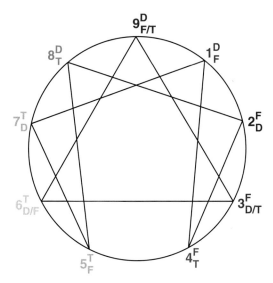

FIGURE 5.1 Enneagram with dominant and support dimensions.

is clearly most obvious for a Two, but the doing support center undergirds the dominant dimension and helps prop it up. As instinctive feelers, Twos receive information with their heart and then immediately respond with their hands. Doing serves as a response to feeling for a Two.

Taking in information with feelings and then responding by doing is what makes it difficult for Twos to say no to people. A dear friend of mine does this day in and day out. She takes in information with her heart and responds with her hands. She senses other peoples' needs and in feeling for them she cannot help but respond with instinctive action as she seeks to offer them care and support. The notion of doing is not quite precise enough here; sometimes her response is inaction. She intuits a sense that moving too fast might hurt someone's feelings, so she freezes. This is still an instinctive, gut-centered response to what her heart has received. The doing center reaction to go slow or to do nothing in response to what her heart takes in is still a common heart then hand reaction from a Two (see Figure 5.2).

Fours. Fours are feeling dominant with a thinking support center. They are a feeling type located near the head triad. This means that Fours feel their feelings deeply and then also analyze their feelings. This fosters the

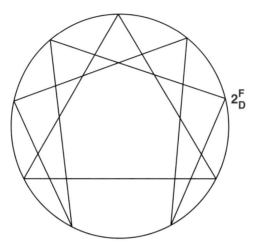

FIGURE 5.2 Type Two: Instinctive Feeler.

creative characteristics we associate with Fours and the common name, the romantic. It also shapes their thoughtful, reflective focus on their own feelings. And, being an analytic feeler fosters their motivating need to make sense of their emotional journey.

A good friend who is a Four has deep thoughts about his feelings in almost every conversation we have. He knows he is heart dominant, aware of how deeply he feels his way through the world trying to find his unique place in it. And then, as quickly as he can name a feeling he can describe it. Feeling, then thinking (see Figure 5.3). This is a reason to see Fours not only as romantics, but as individualists. When he's melancholy, he can write an essay about it. When he's forlorn, he has deep thoughts about why. He knows the difference between these two feelings, and would love to sit and reflect on it with you.

Threes. Threes are also feeling dominant, but you might not know it because of how quickly they displace their feelings. Even though they ignore their feelings, they do unconsciously take in information with the heart, immediately twisting feelings based on a desire to please and impress. Setting their feelings aside, these unemotional feelers ping pong between doing and thinking, typically functioning more like a doer, but with a desire to feel valuable (see Figure 5.4). The performer is a name that shows this doing orientation guided by a misuse of the feeling dimension.

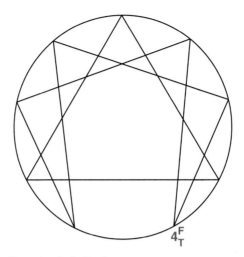

FIGURE 5.3 Type Four: Analytic Feeler.

A fellow Three friend echoes my tendency to never slow down, and to stay active with things that matter more to others than to herself. She has convinced herself that each project matters, but she wrestles and wonders if these efforts to win the approval of her colleagues keeps her from being true to herself. "I see how deceit drives me when I've convinced myself I need to be whatever people want me to be," she recently told me.

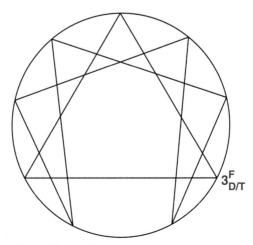

FIGURE 5.4 Type Three: Unemotional Feeler.

Fives. Fives are thinking dominant with feeling as a secondary dimension (see Figure 5.5). Fives are near the bottom of the Enneagram, neighbor to the Four and have some similarities to Fours with their pensive as well as creative traits. However, taking in information with their head means they want to know and understand what is required of them as they make their way in the world and results in them being known as the observer or investigator. As affective thinkers, feeling supports thinking for Fives, which often relates to the attitude Fives have with regard to the focus of their thinking. They are all in with a particular mood related to what is in their heads.

Fives struggle with relationships because they analyze before they feel, but relationships do matter to Fives. They are just more likely to spend time in quiet observation of a relationship rather than directly engaging their feelings or communicating them. A good friend and his co-workers describe his leadership style this way. He is a great team leader but does not necessarily see himself as such. He will say that he knows (in his head) what he wants his working relationships to be, but is not as confident about how to express these things and describes his struggle with how to live them out. He does, however, sometimes expect people to read his mind about what he is thinking as well as feeling.

Sevens. Sevens are also thinking dominant, and their secondary dimension is doing (see Figure 5.6). They neighbor the Eights and that

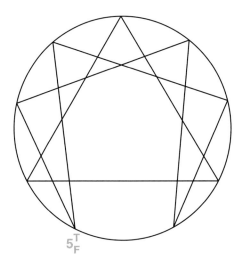

FIGURE 5.5 Type Five: Affective Thinker.

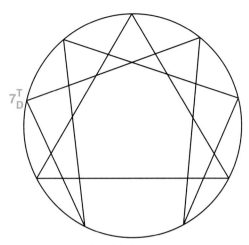

FIGURE 5.6 Type Seven: Instinctive Thinker.

thinking and doing combination gives them a courage to engage others with creative ideas. Sevens, the enthusiasts, always have ideas for what to do next and they bring an optimistic energy to their ideas. This instinctive thinking leads them to be spontaneous and adventurous— ready to act on what comes to mind.

A friend who is a Seven is always upbeat and brings that enthusiasm to each conversation we have. She also brings an idea for a new project or a new direction for our work. "Have you thought about. . ." is often how she begins conversations. Thinking out loud about the possibilities for her department and how to implement them is how she describes her optimistic approach to her team and their work.

Sixes. Sixes are thinking dominant and most Sixes know that overthinking life dominates their experience (see Figure 5.7). At the same time, most Sixes know they also wrestle with the confidence of stating what they truly think about something. Not trusting themselves, these nonrational thinkers connect at a feeling level with others they trust to guide them or they stay busy in the areas where they do have confidence in their knowledge to act. The loyalist is a name that shows the feeling connection and the questioner is a name that reflects the wrestling with thinking.

A close Six friend was asking about COVID-19 vaccinations a couple of years ago. He was reading and wrestling with whether to get the vaccine for himself and his family. He read quite a bit and asked trusted

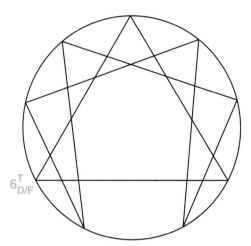

FIGURE 5.7 Type Six: Nonrational Thinker.

friends. Many of us asked a few questions and made our decision; he just could not decide what to do. In the end, he made his decision to get vaccinated not only because so many friends encouraged it, but because he was committed to these friends and felt this was an action to take to support their health as well. He still ended the call with, "Do you think that was right?"

Eights. The Eight is a doing dominant type with thinking as their secondary dimension (see Figure 5.8). Just the reverse of the Seven,

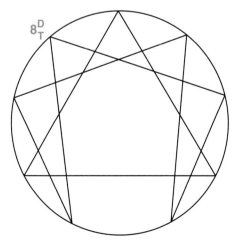

FIGURE 5.8 Type Eight: Analytic Doer.

Eights are also confident and bold, but with less of a focus on big ideas and more of a body dominant desire to be hands on, and to maintain control of whatever situation they find themselves in. Known as the boss, they are actually less interested in controlling others; they just do not want to be controlled by others. These analytic doers are always in motion, acting on the world around them, and thinking about what needs to be done next.

My wife was just saying that her Apple watch thinks she is standing all day, even when she is driving, and she is convinced it is because her whole body is clenched, or engaged, all day every day. Even if it is a problem with the watch, my wife is keenly aware of always being on, and almost always on the move. She does not slow down, and, quoting Pastor Nadia Bolz Weber, she sees that her way of being in the world is "ready, fire, aim." Always ready. Always in action. Thinking follows, so they are ready to act again.

Ones. Ones are doing dominant with a secondary dimension of feeling (see Figure 5.9). They are engaged and active in the world, like Eights, but much more driven by an internal feeling of right and wrong that shapes their action. Their gut prompts them to act, and, while they are not touchy feely, they are passionate about what they are engaged in. These affective doers are emotionally responding to what needs to be done, with strong feelings about the right thing to do in any situation. The result is Ones are known as reformers.

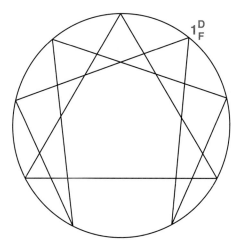

FIGURE 5.9 Type One: Affective Doer.

One of my closest friends is always active, and, as a social worker, is always passionate about her work. More than that, she often asks questions like: "How could anyone not see what is right and wrong in this situation?" She also struggles with burnout, wants to set limits, but also really believes the work is essential and feels that she cannot step away from it.

Nines. Nines are doing dominant, although we don't often see the same energy here as with Eights or Ones. The similarity is not in how much they accomplish, but in the shared desire to be in charge of what they are doing and how it gets done. Nines wrestle with setting priorities and taking action in the moment. Energy seems lacking at times, and in large, part Nines are more comfortable pondering than engaging. Thinking and feeling are the responses we see in Nines as anti-instinctual doers, but it is directly related to their desire to do things on their own terms (see Figure 5.10). Pondering their response to life's demands is where they are most comfortable. The easy-going harmony that Nines seek leads to the name peacemakers.

One of my best friends for many years would disappear in the middle of stressful interactions. One night we were helping her with an important but stressful move she was getting ready to make, and as a Three and an Eight, my wife and I may have pushed too much. The friend snuck

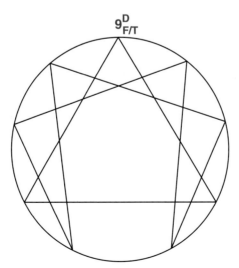

FIGURE 5.10 Type Nine: Anti-Instinctive Doer.

away overwhelmed by it all. My wife, worried about her well-being, went out looking for her. She found her in the grocery store walking the aisles, a safe place to reflect without having to address the challenges awaiting her at home.

DOMINANT-SUPPORT CENTER TEAMS

I want to borrow Hurley and Donson's concept of Dominant-Support Center Teams as a framework to describe my approach to naming how these first two dimensions of our personality work together (Hurley and Donson 1993). These two dimensions, dominant and support, work in tandem for each personality type and we see some similarities between the numbers. There are three such teams: feeling-doing, thinking-feeling, and thinking-doing. The teams are described in the following, and in Table 5.1 we see them all together.

In describing the teams this way, it matters less which dimension is first and more about how the dominant and support work together. Ones and Twos are both on the feeling-doing team even though the order of the two dimensions for a One is doing-feeling and for a Two is feeling-doing. The point is that the One and the Two operate with doing and feeling working in tandem to drive these personality types. Type Sixes do the same thing and are a part of this team because of their mistrust of their thinking dimension. This feeling-doing team focuses on seeing a need and filling a need with a sense of responsibility to make things better. These heart and head types are conscientious and caring. They are comprised of the types I label as Instinctive Feeler (Two), Nonrational Thinker (Six), and Affective Doer (One). What this combination leaves out is confidence in their capacity for thinking.

Table 5.1 Dominant-support teams.

Feeling-Doing Team	Thinking-Feeling Team	Thinking-Doing Team
Instinctive Feeler (Two)	Analytic Feeler (Four)	Unemotional Feeler (Three)
Nonrational Thinker (Six)	Affective Thinker (Five)	Instinctive Thinker (Seven)
Affective Doer (One)	Anti-Instinctive Doer (Nine)	Analytic Doer (Eight)
Thinking repressed	Doing repressed	Feeling repressed

The thinking-feeling team is oriented inwardly, on their own life and making sense of it within themselves. A Four feels first and a Five thinks first, but both of these, and the Nine, function with thinking and feeling working in tandem to drive their personality. This team includes the Analytic Feeler (Four), Affective Thinker (Five), and Anti-Instinctive Doer (Nine). This team is reluctant to engage their doing dimension.

The final team is the thinking-doing team, a combination that leads these types to focus on their own ideas and to believe they can do whatever is needed in response to life. This team is the Unemotional Feeler (Three), Instinctive Thinker (Seven), and Analytic Doer (Eight), and they struggle to see value in feelings.

Each of us has the ability to engage feeling, thinking, and doing more fully, and yet we subconsciously default to a combination of two dimensions with a struggle to engage the third. As we have seen here and in Table 5.2, one of the dimensions drives our personality, and a second dimension supports the work of the dominant one. This support center props up the first, reinforces it, and tilts our personality a certain way that leaves out the third dimension.

The third dimension being held back in our personality hinders the growth that is needed as we seek to be a more balanced person. The way we subconsciously prioritize our capacity for feeling, thinking, and doing is different for each of the nine types, and so is the way we subconsciously repress the third dimension. In the next chapter, we focus more directly on what it means for one of the three to be repressed, how that shapes our personality, and how we can learn from it to bring the dimensions into balance.

Table 5.2 Enneagram dominant and support dimensions.

Type	Dominant Dimension	Support Dimension	Team
Two	Feeling	Doing	Feeling-Doing
Three	Feeling	Doing/Thinking	Doing-Thinking
Four	Feeling	Thinking	Feeling-Thinking
Five	Thinking	Feeling	Feeling-Thinking
Six	Thinking	Feeling/Doing	Feeling-Doing
Seven	Thinking	Doing	Doing-Thinking
Eight	Doing	Thinking	Doing-Thinking
Nine	Doing	Thinking/Feeling	Feeling-Thinking
One	Doing	Feeling	Feeling-Doing

CHAPTER SIX

THE REPRESSED DIMENSION RESULTING IN ENNEAGRAM STANCES

As part of a local election a few years ago, educational leaders and social workers successfully lobbied for revenue to make behavioral interventions in a local school district more equitable in terms of race, and to improve social and emotional learning outcomes. Local district leaders asked my faculty to design several strategies, and along the way, there was the all-too-common threat that the district would need to shift funding away from these commitments. In efforts consistent with my personality as a Three, I would not take no for an answer. I fought for our program, and for what we knew would benefit the diversity of children and their families served by the district.

The local paper called me a "fierce collaborator" during those deliberations. In the midst of pushing for what I felt was needed, my friends and colleagues probably described me as assertive. That is the language commonly used in Enneagram teaching for types Three, Seven, and Eight when we know what we want and always believe we can find a way to make it happen. We are said to have an assertive stance.

What is a stance? We may think of the word in terms of posture and position. A defensive stance in sports is something most athletes can quickly identify: knees bent, feet apart, and hands up. Maybe we think of a stance as a perspective we take, like a social arrangement or a political point of view. For example, I can describe how we took a stance against bullying in our schools. In terms of the Enneagram, we can think of a stance in a similar way. From the perspective of our personality, people see us a certain way. They recognize how we tend to interact socially. What people might recognize in us when we are at our best is someone balanced in our ability to feel, and think, and do; however, too often that is not the case.

Suzanne Stabile uses the analogy of a three-legged stool to highlight our wobbly stance in the struggle to find balance within. Imagine yourself sitting on the three-legged stool of your personality, with thinking, feeling, and doing representing the three legs. At our best, the legs are balanced, and we interact with friends, family, and colleagues from this perspective. However, we are not always at our best; we are wobbly in our personality, and it is the result of one leg being too long and another being too short. One dimension of our personality is dominant in a way that drives our personality and another is repressed, under-utilized, or misused altogether. We may like to see ourselves as balanced or to pretend we are in control of our personality, but the wobble people see is due to the ways we fall asleep to our personality and let these characteristics control us.

THE REPRESSED DIMENSION

I have been building on the work of Hurley and Donson to show how one of the three dimensions of our personality is dominant for each of the nine types and a second dimension supports the automatic responses of the dominant one. We now turn to the third dimension at work within us and what it means for this dimension to be repressed. It may take some convincing that for your Enneagram number, one of the three dimensions is repressed. We must recognize, however, that none of us balance all three centers as well as we might imagine. And certainly not all of the time.

As previously mentioned in the last chapter, this third dimension is not merely least preferred. Because two of these dimensions attempt to do the work of all three, our personality convinces us we do not need the third dimension to function. We have become convinced it is not important in relationships, for our leadership, or in how we make our way through life. To make sense of this, I have designed the following visual images to show how one of the dimensions is all but missing from our personality, and then I turn to talk about the impact this has on the function of our personality. Learning to see this radical imbalance is the most essential work of the Enneagram. Only in making this clear can we take next steps in becoming the leader we want to be.

In terms of organization, I began by introducing the triads with their focus on a dominant center, with a heart-dominant, feeling triad comprised of Two, Three, and Four; a head dominant, thinking triad with Five, Six, and Seven; and a hands dominant, doing triad of Eight, Nine, and One. Now we turn to look at the stances as an alternative organization of the Enneagram based on the dimension that is repressed for each Enneagram type. These do not follow around the Enneagram as neatly, but there is a pattern starting with a number on the core triangle (Three, Six, and Nine) and two types directly across from it. The three feeling repressed types are Three, Seven, and Eight. The thinking repressed types are Six, One, and Two. The doing repressed types are Nine, Four, and Five (see Figures 6.1 and 6.2).

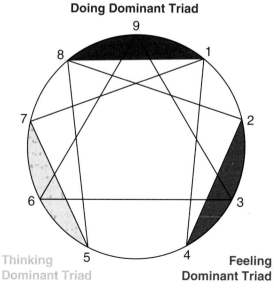

FIGURE 6.1 Image of triads.

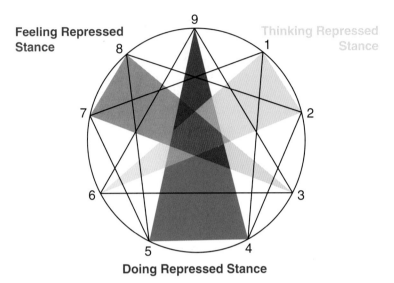

FIGURE 6.2 Image of stances.

COLOR BY NUMBER

In Chapter 2, I mentioned that the three dimensions of personality function like the primary colors in a color wheel, where red, yellow, and blue interact in different ways to create all the colors of the rainbow, all the colors of a large box of Crayola Crayons, and all the thousands of colors in the pantone spectrum. Likewise, feeling, thinking, and doing interact in ways that shape the nine Enneagram types. Just as every color is a combination of red, yellow, and blue, every personality type is a combination of feeling, thinking, and doing. We are all different and unique in some way, and at the same time, we are all combinations of these three dimensions. For the sake of this analogy, let's assign red to feeling, yellow to thinking, and blue to doing. When we are at our best and able to balance these dimensions in ourselves, there is a balance of red, yellow, and blue. Figure 6.3 shows how red, yellow, and blue are all ideally in balance for each of us.

However, because our personality prioritizes these three dimensions in different ways, the colors are out of balance within us. Let's consider what this means for each of the nine types. Following is a description of the ordering of the three dimensions within each of the nine Enneagram types. With each, a graphic shows how the imbalance of the dimensions

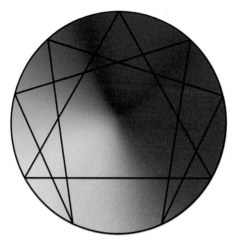

FIGURE 6.3 Personality with dimensions in balance.

shifts the color variations within each personality. As has been the case with Three, Six, and Nine, we consider them last.

For Twos, the order in which the three dimensions are prioritized is feeling, doing, and then thinking. This means Twos are feeling dominant; doing supports feeling, and thinking is repressed. More specifically, their feeling orientation is outwardly focused, and doing works to reinforce the attention they focus on others. An openness to thinking differently about doing and feeling is a challenge for Twos. In other words, if they perceive a need and believe they must respond in a certain way, it is difficult for them to think a different action is acceptable.

As a result, if red is feeling, it is focused in the direction of doing, supported by blue, so that these two interact and there is a less clear thinking (yellow) presence. The red bleeds into the other colors, the red and blue interact, and the yellow is least visible. The image for a type Two is designed to show how red dominates the presence of the other two colors. In Figure 6.4, we see that red is the most pronounced color. Blue is also clear, yet red and blue interact to give a strong violet color next to the red. The red dominates the yellow, making it appear orange. There is only a faint presence of yellow.

For Fours, the arrangement is feeling, thinking, and then doing. Fours are driven by feelings from an internal perspective, and this is reinforced by thinking, with less comfort engaging their doing center. Red is still predominant, but now in the direction of yellow, with less blue presence.

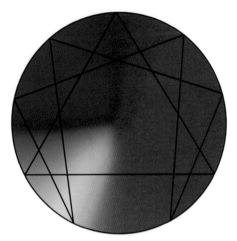

FIGURE 6.4 Type Two (feeling, doing, thinking).

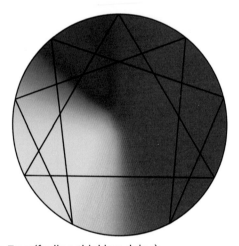

FIGURE 6.5 Type Four (feeling, thinking, doing).

Figure 6.5 shows red as dominant over the other two colors. Red is the most pronounced color. Yellow is also clear, yet red and yellow interact to give a strong orange color next to the red. The red also dominates the blue making it appear light purple. Here, there is only a faint presence of blue.

Fives arrange the dimensions in the order of thinking, feeling, and then doing. Feeling and thinking are the reverse of the Four, but both have doing last. Fives are driven by internalized thinking, reinforced by feeling, with less capacity for the energy of doing. Yellow is now predominant, focused in the direction of red, also with less blue. In Figure 6.6, we see

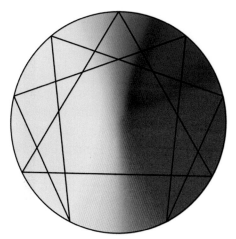

FIGURE 6.6 Type Five (thinking, feeling, doing).

how yellow dominates the presence of the other two colors. Yellow is now the most pronounced color. Red is also clear, yet red and yellow interact to give a strong orange color next to the yellow. The yellow also dominates the blue making it appear green. As a result, any presence of blue is limited.

Sevens are thinking, doing, feeling. Sevens are external thinkers, with more support from doing something with their ideas, and less connection to feeling. Yellow remains predominant, focused in the direction of blue, with less red. Figure 6.7 is designed to show how yellow is dominant over

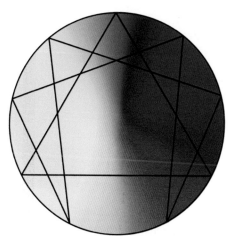

FIGURE 6.7 Type Seven (thinking, doing, feeling).

the other two colors. Yellow is the most pronounced color. Blue is also clear, yet yellow and blue interact to give a strong green color next to the yellow. The yellow also dominates the red making it appear orange. There is only a limited amount of red.

Eights are doing, thinking, feeling. They are doing dominant, with an external focus and support from thinking that rationalizes their actions, and less engaged with feelings. Blue is now dominant, with support from yellow and less red. The image for type Eight in Figure 6.8 shows how blue dominates the presence of the other two colors. Blue is the most pronounced color. Yellow is also clear, yet blue and yellow interact to give a strong green color next to the blue. The blue dominates the red, making it appear violet. There is only a faint presence of red.

Ones are arranged as doing, feeling, and then thinking. They are doing dominant with strong feelings about what and how to do things; it is more difficult to think critically or openly about other possibilities. Blue is dominant and red supports it, with less yellow presence. Figure 6.9 provides an image for type One where blue is dominant compared to the other two primary colors. Blue is most pronounced; red is also clear, yet blue and red interact to give a strong violet color next to the blue. The blue dominates the yellow making it appear green. There is only a limited yellow presence.

As has been the case in discussions throughout this book, the middle numbers of the core triangle in the Enneagram are structured differently. For them, the dominant center that drives their personality is most

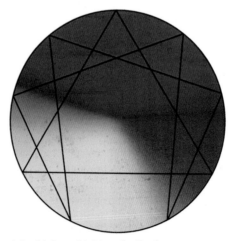

FIGURE 6.8 Type Eight (doing, thinking, feeling).

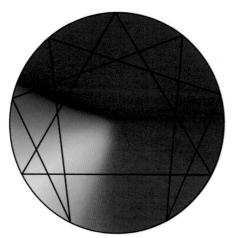

FIGURE 6.9 Type One (doing, feeling, thinking).

misused. We often say this center is dominant and repressed, that it is overused and under-used. It may be better to think of these types as having one dimension that is most present, and at the same time, least well utilized.

For Threes, the dimension that is dominant and repressed is feeling. Threes interact with others based on a need to manage image, which is a misuse of the feeling center. As I said earlier, I worry about how other people feel about me. In this, the support centers are thinking and doing working in tandem, and the genuine use of feelings is often set aside, or repressed, as feelings subconsciously overwhelm threes. Red should be clearer for threes, but it is muted by blue and yellow, feeling is overshadowed by doing and thinking. The image for type Three, see Figure 6.10, shows how red can be dominant and repressed with more clarity of yellow and blue than red.

For Sixes, thinking is the repressed and dominant dimension. Sixes have active minds full of questions and possibilities, but can realize that a full and active mind is not the quiet, open mind needed for clear thinking. Sixes function as feelers connecting loyally to people around them where they seek support, and as doers are able to act on their fears, but in ways that reflect the uncertainty when they cannot quiet their minds. Yellow is not as clear in Sixes, overshadowed by red and blue as thinking is by feeling and doing. As shown in Figure 6.11, type Six shows how yellow can be dominant and repressed with more clarity of red and blue than yellow.

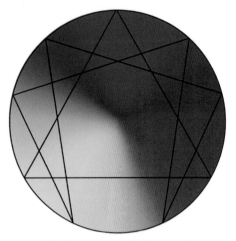

FIGURE 6.10 Type Three (feeling, doing/thinking, feeling).

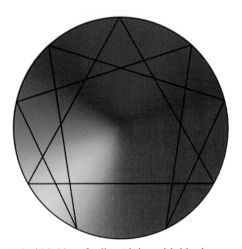

FIGURE 6.11 Type Six (thinking, feeling/doing, thinking).

For Nines, doing is both repressed as well as dominant. Nines can sense a need for action, but their pondering mind and desire for harmonious connection clouds their ability to sense their gut calling them to action. Thinking and feeling are more obvious than doing, which takes a commitment to exerting energy that nines choose to preserve. They withdraw their doing energy and prefer thinking and feeling. Blue is not as clear for Nines with red and yellow more obvious, as shown in Figure 6.12. The image for type Nine shows how blue can be dominant and repressed with more clarity of red and yellow than blue.

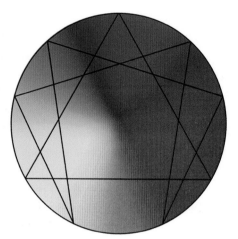

FIGURE 6.12 Type Nine (doing, thinking/feeling, doing).

NAMING THE STANCES

What are the implications of this focus on the dimension that is least obvious in our personality? This center of intelligence that shows up in the third place is what Hurley and Donson (1993) describe as the repressed center. Not only is it in third place, but the first two dimensions work together, overfunctioning, with the third truly lagging behind in terms of how it functions. The result is that for each of us, two dimensions seek to carry out the functions of all three. These two are overemphasized leaving one under-utilized. In reference to the preceding colors, one color is least obvious for each type with the other two providing the distinct tone of that type.

The implication of this ordering, or subconscious prioritizing of the three dimensions, is that certain patterns of behavior can be seen depending on which of the three centers is dominant in one's personality and which is repressed in one's personality. We have considered the dominant center in looking at the triads in the last chapter; here, we are considering impact of the repressed dimension of our personality in creating the groupings known as the stances.

These patterns and the names of these groupings are from the integration of Karen Horney's psychological writings with the Enneagram teachings on the three centers. Horney writes about psychological tendencies, personality-related trends that we exhibit when faced with anxiety, or in her words, *neurotic needs* (Horney 1950). She builds on Walter Cannon's "fight versus flight" by adding a dimension of fright. She also describes these as ways in which we move against, move toward, or move away from others and named them expansive, self-effacing, and resigning solutions, respectively.

Later, when connected to the Enneagram, Horney's three social-psychological tendencies came to be known as aggressive, dependent, and withdrawing dimensions of our personality. Hurley and Dobson (1991) describe these as the three approaches to problem-solving: "seeking expansive solutions in an *aggressive* way, seeking temperate solutions in a *dependent* way, and seeking enlightened solutions in a *withdrawing* way." The result was the aggressive stance that is feeling repressed (made up of the Seven, Eight, and Three), the dependent stance that is thinking repressed (with One, Two, and Six), and the withdrawing stance that is doing repressed (Four, Five, and Nine) (Hurley and Dobson 1991).

Riso and Hudson (2003) have also described these three groupings. They describe them as the three Hornevian Groups, referring to them as assertive, compliant, and withdrawing. When learning about the stance associated with one's personality type, few people like the names associated with these patterns. We tend to want to see the strengths of our personality, forgetting that the patterns of our personality are rooted in a core passion, or struggle, and that our personality is our going down the wrong path as we long for wholeness or our true self. As much as others may like our personality, and as much as we may try to focus on the strengths of it, we have to remember it is also a limited view of who we can be. From this perspective, these three stances are not who we desire to be as leaders, but who we are in our most automatic, habitual, and limited capacity. They represent how we function with the three dimensions of our soul out of balance, and they present a path for how we can work toward balance.

Because people typically do not like the names, I sometimes comment when I am teaching that it is ok if you have a personal reaction to this descriptor—that may help you see part of yourself in a new way. However, I have been learning that while a reaction for personal reasons is something I can accept, I do not want to stand by if there is a reaction for cultural reasons. If being called "aggressive" makes you uncomfortable, that is one thing; if being called "aggressive" reinforces racial stereotypes, particularly for women or people of color, then I want to identify a different language. I have worked harder to listen when students and colleagues suggest not only that "aggressive" feels uncomfortable, but that it also feels racist. As such, I am reverting to *assertive* instead of *aggressive* as Riso and Hudson adopt in *Discovering Your Personality Type* (Riso and Hudson 2003). They often use the terms interchangeably, but I will seek to focus more on the term *assertive*.

Assertive

The Three, Seven, and Eight are the types least connected to the feeling dimension of their personality and they comprise the assertive stance (see Figure 6.13). These numbers do not always perceive of themselves as being assertive, but with some self-reflection, they can see how they come across that way. They do recognize themselves as being positive and upbeat. They are optimistic and believe they can accomplish whatever they set their mind to or address whatever needs to be changed in their world. Hurley and Dobson (1991) say they "desire to restructure, mold, form, and shape the world around them to their liking." This approach to change is a future oriented focus and these numbers find safety and comfort in the future, always anticipating the next opportunity, struggle, or project.

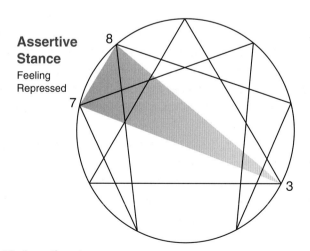

FIGURE 6.13 Assertive stance.

Horney uses the language of "moving against," and this can mean different things for each of these numbers. Threes move against whatever gets in the way of their success-oriented image. Sevens move against anything inhibiting their freedom. Eights move against anything potentially limiting their control. As a result, these types are pushy, at best, or steamrolling, at worst. Such an approach to life and the people around us reflects an inability to center feelings. Addressing feelings is an obstacle to change; considering our own feelings seems like a waste of time. Being assertive is a result of repressing the feeling dimension of our personality. If you are a Three, Seven, or Eight, can you see these characteristics in yourself?

As assertive stance leaders, you may find yourself less comfortable with the emotional aspects of your work. And even when you are able to express or recognize the value of emotion, connecting deeply to the feelings associated with them takes work. Assertive leaders may be loud and direct, but their avoiding of feelings may make them quiet and private as a way of avoiding their feelings and decreasing emotional connection. The unconscious drive to reshape the conditions of work to be what you need or want resonates with most assertive leaders. These leaders have seemingly boundless energy, avoid any sense of weakness, and always have a plan or strategy for what's next. For Threes, it may be the next project (or the next 4–5 projects) as they seek to avoid failure. For Sevens, it may be the next career opportunity or energizing activity, anything that helps them avoid pain. Eights are preparing for the next conflict or crisis, anticipating how to avoid weakness or betrayal.

"Mommy, are you always mad when you work?" The daughter of a colleague, who is an Eight, asked this after observing her mother on several Zoom calls during the pandemic. The mother stopped and reflected on her day, she could not think of a specific instance of being angry at someone that day. Was she direct? Was she urging others to adopt priorities for our school? Was she assertive? She knew her Enneagram type and knew these things to be true, but on this day when observed by her daughter, she did not see herself as being angry. She laughed in hindsight and wondered what her daughter would have thought if she had seen her the day before when she knew she had been angry.

As a Three, I love the way I can interact with this colleague. We never feel like we are hurting each other's feelings. We can be as direct as we want. We spur each other on and get a lot accomplished. However, we know this is not how the rest of our colleagues work. We are both learning to slow down, to pay attention to how we affect others, and to take note of our own feelings regarding some of the challenges we face at work. After a particularly difficult week recently, she sent me the nicest note. It is rare for assertive types to tune in to their feelings and the feelings of others, but when these strong and determined leaders slow down to do this, it makes quite an impact on the culture of their workplace.

Dependent

The dependent stance is made up of Six, One, and Two, and these are the numbers least in touch with their thinking self (see Figure 6.14). This has nothing to do with the intelligence of these types. Rather, it is a reflection on how they approach thinking and the ways they engage others as part of their thinking through things that matter most to them. Hurley and Dobson (1991) describe the desire of these types to know what others are doing in order to help them decide what to do next, and how this is rooted in a desire to be in social relationship with others. It is in the present moment that thinking in a dependent way takes place and these numbers find safety and comfort in the here and now.

From Horney, we use the language of "moving toward" and dependent types utilize an external point of reference, which they move toward. Ones move toward that which will help them be good and act with integrity. Twos move toward others for connection and affection. Sixes move toward those who can reinforce their need for safety. Similarly, Riso and

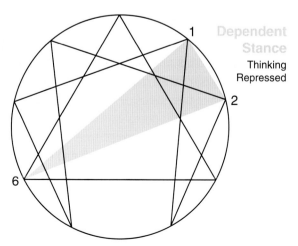

FIGURE 6.14 Dependent stance.

Hudson (2003) have described this stance as compliant, recognizing Ones as compliant to their ego ideal of being good, Twos of being empathetic and helpful, and Sixes as loyal and supportive in seeking their own security and support.

These types are often seen as loyal and responsible. They may see themselves as dependable rather than dependent, but it can be difficult for them to sort out their own thoughts, or they may rely on underdeveloped ideas, or opinions, rather than critical thinking that allows them to be open to new and different ideas. Their approach to thinking often rationalizes or reinforces the ideas that are most comfortable to them.

This can also lead dependent stance types to overthink things, which is not clear and objective thinking, but rather it is letting their mind run with ideas that can overwhelm them. A friend who is a Two describes the regular occurrence of "analysis paralysis" in overthinking most decisions he makes. Being dependent is a result of repressing the thinking dimension of our personality. If you are a Six, One, or Two, can you see how this is true for you?

Dependent stance leaders value hard work and responsibility, they wrestle with the anxiety of their work, and they struggle to set boundaries. When they do set boundaries, it can be an all or nothing boundary because negotiating risks feelings and requires thinking. Planning ahead requires additional work for these leaders. It is easier to engage in what the present moment means to your work. Likewise, they may also value the work of the moment more since future planning seems abstract and impersonal. In focusing on the immediate, Ones are committed to what needs to be done right now, avoiding frustration in making their own mistakes as well as the mistakes of the people and systems that surround them. Twos focus on what the person right in front of them requires of them, and, in thinking about relationships, they seek to avoid their own needs and neediness. Sixes are concerned with the responsibilities of their schedule and avoiding unpredictable uncertainties that bring doubt to their work. Others may be setting the agenda for dependent stance leaders, so they may not be able to celebrate their accomplishments or trust the accolades of work well done.

A colleague who is a department leader once asked not to chair an important committee in our school where fellow faculty regularly had strong feelings about the agenda items. I tried to counsel her to just move through the agenda and not to let the feelings of others weigh her down.

It was as if I was speaking another language. Another leader joined the conversation, and they both shared that managing the people was as weighty to them in their leadership as the work at hand. The tasks of their roles were quite feasible, and left to their own or with enough time, they could excel. They preferred working with people, but the feelings of the people and the tasks of the agenda flowed together in such a way that they could not easily think through how to separate them and only focus on what needed to be accomplished. The presence of other people was a gift to them, but it also clouded their thinking in the moment.

Withdrawing

The withdrawing stance includes the Nine, Four, and Five types, and they are least connected to their doing dimension (see Figure 6.15). They may be active, but can be more easily overwhelmed by external pressures. They pay attention to the energy that is required of them to be active and engaged. They are independent in terms of their thinking and feeling, but they doubt they can change the reality of the world around them and are unsure that it would be worth the energy. Hurley and Dobson (1991) describe this as a self-protective approach to life as they retreat within themselves to find a way through life.

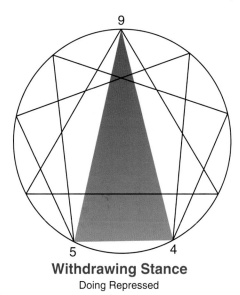

Withdrawing Stance
Doing Repressed

FIGURE 6.15 Withdrawing stance.

Withdrawing types go inward to find fulfillment and in line with Horney, they "move away from" life's challenges. Fours move away from what reminds them that something may be lacking; Fives, from what reminds them they may not be competent or prepared; and Nines, from what might disrupt their peace or create conflict. As they look within, they prefer nostalgia and have a preference for looking back to how things were. They find comfort and safety in the past when things were easier or they knew what was required of them. Being withdrawn is a matter of repressing the doing dimension of one's personality. If you are a Nine, Four, or Five, can you recognize these tendencies within yourself?

Leaders in the withdrawing stance are focused on what they want to do more so than what needs to be done or what others are requiring them to do. They have a reference point within themselves, so they are looking within for guidance and confidence. The internal focus, and the engagement of their own thoughts and feelings takes a lot of energy—it is doing something. It is just not the kind of doing others expect of them. What keeps their focus from whatever else is required of them? Fours are focused on what is missing in their life, and long to avoid that which is commonplace or ordinary. Fives focus on the information they have and what more is required, avoiding situations where they don't know what might be expected of them. Nines can feel powerless when they doubt their leadership matters; making a decision may bring conflict, which they are seeking to avoid at all times.

"I teach civic education and I never vote. I just don't think my vote makes a difference." Too many Americans feel this way, but there is something about a type Nine who is known as a leader in their field saying this. We were talking about Enneagram messages, and she described how her own resignation and reluctance were reflections of her struggle to do the very things she believes are important.

A Four was talking about being annoyed by a particular office on his campus and a new technology they implemented. He was frustrated it did not work more smoothly and he needed that office to help him finish some end of semester responsibilities. "Do they understood how hard they make things for people?" he asked. He talked about not being valued by them and how personal it felt. He knew he could call them and get some help, but hadn't done so. I asked him about his next step and he talked more about feeling unseen. He finally exclaimed, "It's just so hard to do things!" We all feel that way at times, but prioritizing the actions they need to do is just a little more work for the withdrawing stance types.

The following table lists the Enneagram stances.

Assertive Stance
Under-reliance on the heart function/feeling repressed
Pursue their own agenda first
Move against others
Expressive but not emotional
Strive to reshape people or situations
Future-oriented
Stress response is to fight
Enneagram types Three, Seven, and Eight
Dependent Stance
Under-reliance on the head function/thinking repressed
Concerned with others' expectations
Move with others
Loyal, responsible, and dependable
Demonstrate nonproductive thinking and overthinking
Present-oriented
Stress response is fright
Enneagram types One, Two, and Six
Withdrawing Stance
Under-reliance on the gut function/doing repressed
Slow to act
Move away from others
Motivated to do what they want when they want
Past-oriented
Stress response is flight
Enneagram types Four, Five, and Nine

The three dimensions of human functioning that make us who we are, our capacity for feeling, thinking, and doing, are never fully in balance in our approach to the world. We have seen how for each of the nine Enneagram types, one of these dimensions is dominant, a second supports the dominant dimension, and a third is far less engaged in the work of our personality. In other words, we subconsciously prioritize one and repress another. I have presented the order of the dimensions for each type and then shown the organization that results when three types repress feeling, three repress thinking, and three repress doing. The results are the assertive, dependent, and withdrawing stances of the Enneagram.

Now that we know this, what does it mean for our leadership? And, because it is so descriptive of how we are, rather than prescriptive for how we ought to lead, what do we learn from this about how to develop as leaders? The next chapter focuses more in depth on the implications of the stances for each of the nine types. What more can each type learn about themselves and what keeps their repressed center from being more fully developed?

Then we learn to develop the balance we long for as we lead. Let us look within each number and how each functions in light of the stance it falls in. The patterns of being assertive, of being dependent, or of being withdrawn reflect the imbalance of the three centers. However, our personality is dynamic and there are pathways to growth and transformation within us to expand the leadership we offer. Let us turn now to seeing the imbalance of our own type more clearly and to seeking balance in our soul.

The next table shows each of the dimensions for each type: dominant, support, and repressed, and the stance name for the patterns reflecting the repressed dimension.

Type	Dominant Dimension	Support Dimension	Repressed Dimension	Stance
Two	Feeling	Doing	Thinking	Dependent
Three	Feeling	Doing/Thinking	Feeling	Assertive
Four	Feeling	Thinking	Doing	Withdrawing
Five	Thinking	Feeling	Doing	Withdrawing
Six	Thinking	Feeling/Doing	Thinking	Dependent
Seven	Thinking	Doing	Feeling	Assertive
Eight	Doing	Thinking	Feeling	Assertive
Nine	Doing	Thinking/Feeling	Doing	Withdrawing
One	Doing	Feeling	Thinking	Dependent

UNIT THREE

The final unit helps us apply the knowledge of how the dimensions function for our personality type. Now that you know your number, and now that you know which dimension is dominant for you, which dimension supports your dominant dimension, and which is most repressed in your personality, we have to be willing to slow down and look for how these characteristics are at work within us. This begins with an invitation to wake up to your personality and how it drives you.

Perhaps you can look back and see examples of how these dimensions have been out of balance in your life and as you lead. Have you also learned to see this in the moment? Enneagram wisdom, or what I describe as becoming stancewise, is learning to catch your personality in the act. It is learning to see the imbalance in the moment when you are reluctant to keep your thinking open to a different idea, hesitant to sit with your feelings as you are feeling them, or unwilling to act on an impulse that seems right, but requires energy.

In developing this wisdom by recognizing the imbalance as you lead, stancework is the process of observation, listening, and allowing new and different responses that are less mechanical and more intentional as you seek balance. Developing open hearts, open heads, and open hands helps to nurture this balance and grow our soul; this is the work that is essential for becoming the leaders we desire to be.

The work of seeing ourselves more clearly and nurturing wisdom for growth requires intentional practices. Waking up to these things is the work of mindfulness. The final chapter introduces several Enneagram practices for fostering the wisdom required of us to be effective as we lead.

CHAPTER SEVEN

STANCEWISE
Enneagram Wisdom by the Number

Have you ever been driving down the highway and all of sudden you see a mile marker that is 10 miles farther down the journey than the last time you remember paying attention to the road? I know I am not the only one! I was taking a Defensive Driving class a year ago (don't worry—I wasn't driving that fast) and I heard the concept: highway hypnosis. I didn't know there was a name for this. I did know there's a band called "Asleep at the Wheel." Maybe this is a bigger problem than we realize!

And, while it may be most dangerous when we are driving, tuning out of the present moment happens all the time—and as leaders we are not immune. It happens in meetings, it happens in conversations, it happens when you want to focus on a task, but the distractions take over. We all fall asleep to what is happening in the moment and must learn to see this as an invitation to wake up and to see ourselves more clearly.

Now that we know the names of the Enneagram stances and some characteristics of these three ways of being in the world, I want to return to each Enneagram type with a little more detail and a focus on how our stacking of the three dimensions influences our leadership. We have each prioritized these three dimensions over the course of a lifetime, albeit completely subconsciously, and we cannot simply choose to reorder them. We must first learn to see the extent to which this ordering keeps our personality asleep or on autopilot and then seek balance among these dimensions as they function within us.

Your stance is determined by which of the three dimensions is repressed, functioning at its lowest level, unconsciously, and on auto-pilot. We are asleep to the ways all three of the dimensions are at work within us, but the repressed dimension is functioning at its lowest capacity and we have no idea. There is a deep sleep that keeps us from engaging that part of our personality. Assertive stance personalities do not want to hear that we engage our feelings at the lowest level. Dependent stances do not want to hear they are thinking repressed. A Withdrawing type is usually content with their level of doing. And yet, to those around us the degree of imbalance of the three dimensions is obvious and the ways we are asleep to our repressed center can be detrimental in our relationships and our work together.

Much of Gurdjieff's work was focused on the need to wake up to the ways we are going through the world completely unaware of the control our personality has on our life. It happens most when stress is taking its toll on us and when we are feeling overwhelmed by life's demands. When this happens, we are distracted by the focus of this concern and we lose sight of the present moment. It happens to me in meetings on a regular basis. I have to catch myself and ask: Am I really listening? Or am I focused on the decision I plan to make? Or on the next meeting?

Are you aware of how you function on autopilot? At work? In relationships? How are you unaware of your personality getting in the way? Of your repressed dimension having fallen asleep?

Because we are asleep to these kinds of experiences, we each need a wake-up call. Riso and Hudson created a wake-up call for each Enneagram type (Riso and Hudson 1999). Each type specific wake-up call is an invitation to see how you are falling asleep to these things and how your lack of awareness reinforces the power of your stance-related characteristics. The wake-up call is a recognition of those inner urgings each number has to protect their ego ideal. The wake-up call is an invitation to see how your personality is in control of you rather than you being in control of it.

In this chapter, I walk through each Enneagram type by stance looking at the ordering of the three dimensions and how the wake-up call for each number can be an opportunity to see these things within yourself—a call to wake up!

Tony De Mello was an Indian Jesuit priest and author of *Awareness*, a foundational precursor to the contemporary field of mindfulness. He often led talks about the ways we fall asleep, zone out, and get lost in thought in all kinds of situations. He was a meek and mild teacher with a steady, calming voice. And as he tells these convicting but inspiring stories, he would get to a certain point in his speeches, take a pause, and scream, "WAKE UP!" It was startling and that was the point. You can't hear me yelling at you, but I do hope these insights help us wake up to our personalities and the power our Enneagram stance has over us. Furthermore, I hope the suggestions and guidance for each type provided here brings value to the self-awareness we are developing as leaders.

DEPENDENT STANCE

Ones

Ones often see their purpose as a leader focused on making the world a better place. Their top priorities are focused on their sense of responsibility for their work and have a focus on the need to improve everything around them. They feel deeply about what they do and how they do it.

Needing to be right combined with a strong sense of obligation to improve things are reflective of a strong doing center and a repressed thinking center, as shown again in Figure 7.1. Ones struggle with objectively asking if the task at hand is theirs to fix or if their approach is the best way. They have strong feelings about the way they approach change, but that is not the same as having critically thought through the options.

Even using the idea of "critical thinking" is risky with a One in that they are usually very aware of the ways they criticize thoughts and actions. Critical thinking, however, is not about the criticism Ones offer. It is not about the strong feelings they have. It is certainly not about the inner critical voice that is always correcting them. That harsh inner voice is not

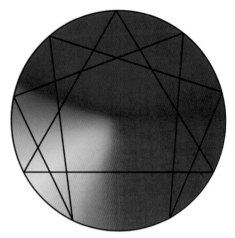

FIGURE 7.1 Ones: How does the strong feeling to do the right thing limit your openness to new ideas?

thinking at all, but rather it is simply the noise that fills the mind of a One. Thinking requires a quiet mind, an open mind. Critical thinking is the ability to approach something with some openness and objectivity and this is more difficult for a One, whose mind may be made up about what is right and what is wrong before taking in any additional information.

Ones must develop critical thinking or the ability to evaluate themselves and their work more objectively when their default is to over-evaluate or over-analyze, which tends to reinforce their need to act with integrity to be good and right. For a One, to listen to how they feel about what they want to do is essential, but this is not the same as thinking. Ones always feel strongly about how they do things. Ones must sit with the feelings they have about the need to improve, to be correct, or to do more. What is that feeling like? How does it feel? These are more helpful to ask than why a One feels a certain way.

Asking why they feel something helps explain a feeling, but that does not help the One productively engage in feeling or in thinking. This is a part of what Stabile (2018) means when she teaches that Ones do not engage in "productive thinking." Thinking requires setting boundaries on their expectations and on the projects in which they are involved. It means saying no. It means exploring other options and possibilities for action. Unlike a Two, they are not saying yes to work for the sake of the relationships, but for the sake of improving work. That can be helpful for the One and for those of us who work with Ones; however, more questions must be considered about the nature of the improvement that has captured their attention and kept the response of their personality on autopilot.

The wake-up call for a type One is their perceived obligation to improve things and to do so a certain way. This strong urge can alert a One to their autopilot approach to taking on improvement projects, judging work that is not done to their standard, and being overly critical of their work and the work of others. If they do not wake up to these things, the passion of resentment takes over. As internalized doers, this passion is focused inward first, then toward others. The resentment will distract from the path to serenity, the virtue of the Ones. The resentment keeps their body's response tight and tangled in knots. It does not allow for a calm, peace-filled balanced response.

I have mentioned how each stance moves in a certain direction. "Moving toward" is the directional language guiding dependent stance numbers. In describing what it means for Ones to be in the dependent stance, to be thinking repressed, Jocelyn Campbell (2012) offers that Ones unconsciously move toward whatever will help them earn an internal sense of righteousness, integrity, and autonomy. Ones may think that they are thinkers, but as Hurley and Donson (2000) say, the automatic or habitual move to do what they feel is good or right reinforces opinions more than it reflects clear thinking. As a result, in leadership, it is difficult for Ones to manage expectations; they expect too much of themselves, and others. Ones feel that they will never be good enough, right enough, perfect enough, or thorough enough.

How can Ones recognize the feelings they have that reinforce their compulsion to do, to fix, to improve? One suggestion I learned from Rev. Nadia Bolz Weber's church is the goal of being "anti-excellence" and "pro-participation." Similarly, *satisficing* is how organizational scholar Herbert Simon described an approach to decision-making where a satisfactory decision that suffices is optimal even if not ideal (Simon 1957). This is an invitation to be content with decisions without worrying about being right or perfect. It recognizes the value of effort without having to pursue excellence in all things. With this way of thinking, Ones can accept that we are all wrong some of the time and that mistakes are ok.

If you are a One, when you feel compelled to do the right thing, to quickly move to action, your thinking and your feeling tend to be jumbled together and thinking gets left behind. Engaging in thinking means being open to slowing down and asking more questions when you feel responsible for the problems and the need to change everything around you. *Seething* is a word a friend who is a One uses to describe when that inner drive to action takes over. Consider what it will take to be open to a different perspective when you are seething to do what you feel is right, what you believe—not think—is right. As part of this, practice taking breaks, build rest into your day, and know the responsibility of work will be there later. You desire what is good and the pause from work is also a good thing.

When working with or supervising a One, be honest and committed because Ones value these things. Even in times of conflict and when offering criticism, show your commitment to the relationship; their feeling orientation values this level of connection and they want to know that you support them. Their inner voice is criticizing them and their assumption is that you are criticizing them as well. When you do offer criticism, be kind and gentle, and own your own mistakes. This also shows your commitment to them and the value of your work together. While Ones are doers, they do want meaningful and supportive relationships—partnerships—in the work you can be committed to together. When they bring a range of ideas (instead of their one right way) and when they see another side of a situation, that is evidence of thinking through the bigger picture at a higher level and is something to celebrate with Ones.

Twos

Twos in leadership are attuned to what the people in their life are feeling and what they need. They sense what others are feeling and they feel the need to do something about it. This reflects their feeling dominant perspective and the way doing supports feeling. Twos are often named Helpers, which is shorthand for this tendency to do something in response to how they perceive others are feeling, and to do so without critically thinking about whether they need to be the person offering help (see Figure 7.2).

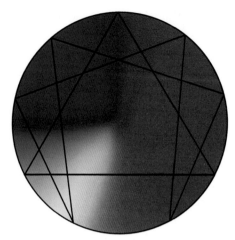

FIGURE 7.2 Twos: How does the desire to nurture relationships keep you from thinking about the importance of setting boundaries?

Their actions are motivated by a need to be needed, making it a real challenge for Twos in leadership to prioritize taking care of themselves. They are constantly focused on others. This can also make it difficult for Twos to focus on activities apart from people. Strategic planning or independent research is often less appealing to Twos. Twos thrive in relational leadership and look for opportunities to nurture interpersonal connection.

As a result, the wake-up call that a Two must recognize is their compulsion to reach out and nurture. It is the drive to win over people by being overly supportive; it is a tendency to say, "Let me do that for you." Twos may ask, "When am I not doing that?" Fair enough! When are you doing it in a way that you are not even aware? When you catch yourself in the act you can ask whether the connection you are nurturing is truly needed in that moment.

It is this overextended belief that their response is needed by people who feel anxious, sad, afraid, worried, or overwhelmed that leads to the Two's passion of pride. It is an externalized feeling orientation that is focused on others. Pride in their ability to feel people's feelings and respond in the most meaningful way prevents the path to humility. Similar to Ones, Twos must develop a clear and open mind where they can seek objectivity with regard to their need to understand and respond to others. To stop and ask if you need to help is an expression of engaging your thinking self.

By repressing thinking, Twos do not adequately question whether their responses are appropriate. As a result, it is difficult for Twos to set boundaries around their desire to be loved. Stabile, herself a Two, often says that Twos like to think of themselves as thinkers, but "You are likely thinking only about 2 things—people and relationships" (Stabile 2018). Twos assume other people need them and that they themselves have very few significant needs; as a result, Twos over-focus on others, over-emphasize a feeling connection, and over-function in relationships.

Twos also move toward others as part of the dependent stance movement. They move toward experiences that will help them earn other people's attention and approval. Ones move internally toward what is right; Twos move externally toward others. This reinforces the need to recognize the wake-up call, the belief that they must go out to others to win them over.

If you are a Two, developing a thinking self may feel completely foreign, or it may feel like something you need to do with others. The hard truth is that it is nearly impossible to do this with others—supporting the people who surround you will remain your focus. You must learn to spend time alone doing something you enjoy. Trust that others are doing fine without your help and that you are still loved.

Twos almost always think they are more direct with others than they actually are. Keep working on being direct about your own needs. Keep working on saying no. Keep setting boundaries and keep asking questions. Do more of each of these things as a way to develop objectivity in your thinking.

When it comes to thinking, Twos have lots of ideas to share. A friend recently asked if I was impressed with all the ideas she had. I was, and I said so. I followed by also suggesting that the work of thinking is also weeding out the ideas, organizing the ideas, expanding on the ideas, and analyzing the ideas. Not just having good ideas. Maybe my response discouraged her, but it did give her a different way to think about thinking.

For those of us who work with Twos, allow time for them to process aloud what they are working on. We have to be patient as they talk through what they are thinking, how they want to respond, and how they set limits and practice saying no. We often want to encourage the helping attributes of a Two. We need to do that, particularly since Twos find it difficult to hear praise, but we also need to honor and recognize the new ideas, questions, and limits that Twos set as part of the balance they are seeking.

Sixes

Sixes are the middle number in the dependent stance, which means the same center is preferred and repressed—thinking. As leaders, Sixes engage the world with their head, needing information, wanting to understand the world around them, but then making sense of what they take in can overwhelm them. They want clarity in understanding what they have taken in, all the while wanting more and more information. They are busy gathering information from people around them, but find it difficult to trust any of it. They struggle to trust what others have given them and they struggle to trust their own understanding of the information they have (see Figure 7.3).

We often say that Sixes overthink, but it is more a matter of spinning the wheels of the mind rather than engaging in meaningful thought processes. What is in their mind is loud and overwhelming, cluttering their head and keeping them questioning their own leadership. It is much more

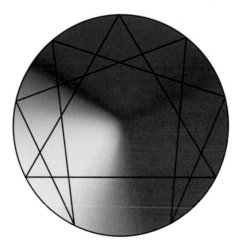

FIGURE 7.3 Sixes: How does the constant questioning prevent you from learning to trust yourself?

difficult for Sixes to foster a quiet mind as they lead. The lack of trust in making sense of what is in their head reinforces opinions they already hold or leads to continual questioning of what they wonder to be true and makes decision-making an ongoing challenge.

The wake-up call for a Six is when this questioning and self-doubt leads to an overdependence on others for guidance and support. When fear and anxiety are intense, so is self-doubt. Sixes want to rely on others but worry about not having support from others. Sixes nurture loyalty as a way to foster a network they can rely on, but the cycle of wanting to rely on others versus not trusting others makes the worry even stronger, reinforcing their passion of fear.

It is clear then that Sixes move toward what will help them earn safety and security. Sixes become dependent on something outside of themselves for guidance. They are trying to overcome the fear associated with all the information they have taken in but cannot find the quiet space needed in their own heads to reassure them. They give in to their fear as they seek outside support to alleviate it.

If you are a Six, you must seek to foster a quiet mind as a way to develop a sense of inner trust and overcome your fear. Look within as you seek to trust yourself. We often talk about dependent stance types as being more present oriented, and while Sixes may feel safer in the present than the unknown future, this does not mean Sixes easily practice mindfulness and being truly aware and grounded in the present moment. As you lead, ask questions, but also allow yourself time to reflect on the questions you ask with an open mind. To which ones do you already know the answer? Can you trust what you know? Trust what you know and practice taking risks without the need for outside assurance or overplanning.

When we work with Sixes in leadership, we have to learn to appreciate the questions they ask. Their questions can be a way for you to think through things with them. Use them as a way to kindly and reassuringly help them answer their questions on their own. Do not tell them to stop worrying or planning or asking questions; let them process their concerns with you in a way that can help them develop self-assurance. Sixes will still want reassurance from others and you can offer that by taking time for caring conversations where you help answer their questions while feeling free to ask them to help answer some on their own.

WITHDRAWING STANCE

Fours

Fours in leadership want to be seen and understood. We often describe the creative and expressive aspects of a Four—characteristics that seek to capture their internally focused feeling orientation. This focus keeps them longing for an expression of who they are and what sets them apart. As leaders, they want to be seen as special, as distinctive, and want to connect with others as a result of these things.

Fours value emotions and personal connections and this leads them to be emotionally sensitive, which is a gift and struggle as they lead. They want to be understood and to understand themselves. They have deep feelings and deep thoughts about their feelings. And, this keeps them in the cycle of feeling and thinking with their doing dimension repressed (see Figure 7.4). Action takes more energy and a sense of commitment that is difficult given the inner turmoil they experience. They may know they have the capacity for leadership, but the ability to sustain it is a challenge. They have a tendency to second-guess their leadership skill or they just want more from their leadership than what they think they can offer. An imagined approach to leadership, a fantasized vision of their leadership keeps them from engaging the skills they have.

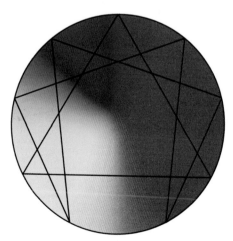

FIGURE 7.4 Fours: How does diving deep into the intensity of your emotions prevent you from engaging in what needs to be done?

The wake-up call for a Four is when they intensify their feelings. It is their belief that no one understands what they want or are trying to do, or who they are. They express a longing for something they feel they do not have. They focus on what is missing. These each keep a Four from acting on their responsibilities as a leader. The desire to be an authentic leader keeps them from being an active leader. In relationships, Fours want to nurture a presence with others, but end up creating distance. As leaders, this same phenomenon occurs. This leads to the passion of envy, of longing, and of believing they are missing out on what they could have, what they could do, or what they could be.

As we turn now to the withdrawing stance, we see Enneagram types who "move away" from leadership responsibility. They move away from meaningful action and focus on finding meaning. They move away from whatever triggers a belief that something in their work is lacking, that something in their being is lacking. And yet, this reinforces a belief that something is lacking. Fours hold on to and intensify their feelings through an imaginary world of the leader they long to be.

If you are a Four, you can learn to be grateful for the opportunities you have, without dreaming of a better situation. When you see yourself wanting more or longing for something different, practice a spirit of gratitude for what you do have. You know you can be intense and that your feelings can overwhelm others, so you can learn to communicate without overwhelming. And when your colleagues respond by seeming overwhelmed, don't retreat away. Stay present, focus on what you are sharing as you lead, on how you communicate, and try to engage in new and different ways even if it doesn't feel as authentic. Your doing dimension matters as much as your feeling and thinking dimensions.

When working with Fours, let them feel their feelings. They may help you nurture your own! You can support the feelings of others without having to feel what they are feeling. Fours may try to pull us in or push us away; our role can be that of a steady presence—not over-engaging the feelings or ignoring them, but acknowledging them. And, then, offer support for what they share and what they are doing. Help Fours see the value of their contributions and of being an active and appreciated leader in your work together.

Fives

The dominant center for Fives is thinking where they interpret the world through their mind with a clear value given to data, logic, and analysis. The world around them is overwhelming, so they observe what surrounds them and take it in to their head. As they take in information, they give value to their ideas and over-identify with them. They have strong feelings about their ideas, but active engagement in implementing their ideas is much more difficult (see Figure 7.5).

Fives repress doing, believing it is almost impossible to change things in the world around them. And even if change is possible, it takes so much work, so much energy. Fives lack the self-assurance that their leadership is as effective as what others might offer.

The wake-up call for Fives is their retreat into their mind and away from the outer world of responsibility. Fives want more time to gather information and to think about decisions. Unlike Sixes, Fives are quite confident in their mind and prefer to stay there rather than seeking connections with others to help guide them. "If I just stick to myself, I can figure it out," says a Five. This is what leads to the passion of avarice, or greed for information.

Fives are tempted to keep exploring as they want to know more and more, which is more comfortable than acting on what they already know.

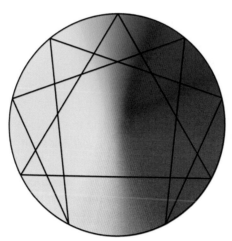

FIGURE 7.5 Fives: How does the focus on understanding the world around you keep you from acting on what others need from you?

They feel competent in their head, far less so in the world around them. Leadership requires action, and action requires work and energy they do not believe they can muster.

As a result, the movement of Fives is away from what triggers a sense of social inadequacy or incompetence in the world around them. Fives withdraw from reality into concepts and mental worlds. This wake-up call is an invitation to engage their doing center, to discern what action is required of them as they seek to be more effective in their leadership.

As a Five, you know what others expect of you. Trust this and take the steps of doing these things. You know what your organization requires of you and you know what you want to see happen in the world. You have studied these things well and now is the time to act. When it feels like the actions are requiring more energy than you can offer, communicate this. Let others know how much you can do and when you can be engaged. This communication is also an act of doing that brings value to your leadership.

For those of us who work with Fives, share the details needed for the work. They need to know the road map and the destination to the greatest extent possible. This helps them feel more confident in themselves, trusting of colleagues, and secure in their work environment. Allow Fives time to reflect and think through their work, and when they are active in responding, offer praise for what they do.

Nines

Nines are another type whose dominant dimension is also their repressed dimension. In their case, as a withdrawing type, the dominant and repressed dimension is doing (see Figure 7.6). As leaders, they see what needs to be done, but prioritizing acting on the tasks that matter most requires an energy they have to work to exert. Nines in leadership will be productive and engaged in doing something; it just will not always be what others need them to do, or on the timeline others expect.

As expectations grow, Nines feel like they don't have the energy to do what the job requires. Or, they believe it just might not be worth their use of the energy they do have. The drive to act is repressed, leading Nines to wonder if their leadership even matters. Just as Sixes want to know things and yet doubt what they do know, resulting in self-doubt, Nines

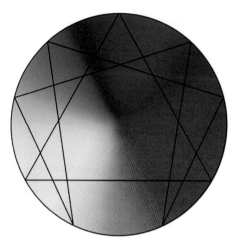

FIGURE 7.6 Nines: How does pondering what others want keep you from expending the energy to act on your priorities?

want to see things changed, they want to see things go a certain way, and even get frustrated when things are not being done. They often struggle to believe the work required is theirs to do and the result is a self-forgetting or self-negation.

The wake-up call for a Nine is when they accommodate themselves to others. It is when they go along to get along. Their devaluing of their own contributions leads them to merge with the will and wishes of others. They may be reluctant to speak their mind, or act on behalf of what they know to be best. They fail to act in ways that are needed resulting in the passion of resignation. As I mentioned earlier, this is not laziness, but a desire to be unaffected by life.

In this, we see that Nines also move away—they move away from what triggers a sense of distress and discomfort. Nines withdraw in the face of potential conflict, when stress is increased, and when the energy required to address such things just feels like it's too much. Nines move away from others' expectations, and they move away from their own inner conflict. They move away from whatever disturbs a sense of inner harmony. A friend recently laughed at the name "peacemaker" used for Nines instead offering "harmony seeker."

Nines, you can find the energy you need to remain productive and experience harmony in yourself and with others. You are aware of the times in your lives when the energy and action required of you was worth it.

You will want to focus on the times it wasn't worth it, but you can also recall the times where it has been. Exert yourself and trust that your active responses as a leader are worth it. Take time to reflect, but also be mindful of that time and how it compares to the time offered in active engagement of your work. And while thinking is work, don't confuse it for the tasks that need to be done.

When working with Nines who lead, understand that they need to see the value and strength of their contributions. Their vision for leadership matters and their contributions matter. Be clear about how their work matters and what is expected of them. Nines may say yes and may even do the work, but this doesn't reflect a commitment on their part. You can help nurture Nines' commitment to the work by discussing its value and asking them to reflect on what it means; this can generate a deeper commitment within them for the work as opposed to asking them to simply say yes to something in which they really are not invested. They will go along to get along unless they work with you to develop a deeper commitment to what they are doing.

ASSERTIVE STANCE

Sevens

Sevens are energetic and talented leaders with many interests. These diverse interests reflect their thinking dominant perspective. They are energetic dreamers, spontaneous, and leaders with an active mind. Sevens work hard, but follow-through by staying on the same task for a long period of time is a challenge. They think about possibilities before them, commit to doing something in response to their ideas, but turn to another new idea for fear of getting stuck having to do the same thing over and over again.

Sevens think about big ideas and are focused on fun and freedom. This is an externally focused thinking: "Have you thought about. . .?" This external expression focused on seeking happiness serves as a way to avoid their fear of an inner sadness. Dealing with sadness requires a sustained connection to feeling, which is the repressed center of this assertive stance. Dismissing the importance of emotions in themselves and in others affects their capacity for leadership (see Figure 7.7).

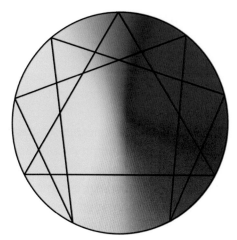

FIGURE 7.7 Sevens: How does thinking about better options for life prevent you from sitting with your real feelings?

Their tendency is to think about feelings, which is not the same as feeling their feelings. When the feelings become too much they turn to the next exciting adventure.

The wake-up call for Sevens is when they find themselves thinking about something better available somewhere else. It is their belief that the grass is greener on the other side. This manifests itself as an impulsiveness that can make a Seven seem out of control. This leads to the passion of gluttony; the compulsive focus on activity to keep their minds free can function like an addiction to help them avoid the anxiety within.

Assertive stance types are known to "move against," and Sevens move against whatever gets in the way of their pursuit of inner satisfaction and freedom. Sevens assert themselves against people and situations that make them feel trapped; they can do this in a way that makes them feel like the life of the party when everyone is on board with their new and exciting ideas, or in a way that makes them suck the life out of the room when they are trying to entertain in a situation where difficult decisions must be made or resolve must be demonstrated to move a project to completion.

When leading, Sevens do not give in to that inner urge to make light of serious situations or escape from pain. Stay present to what is being discussed and the work that is being done, even if it begins to feel mundane.

Let others express what they are feeling even if you think it brings the mood down below where you are comfortable; you will be safe in sitting with these feelings. This is the practice of emotional intelligence and it is essential to your leadership. As part of this, you can also develop the ability to share your own feelings. Even at work, the personal aspects of life matter to how we function. Allow time and space for genuine sharing of personal experiences. The thinking dimension of your leadership overwhelms your feeling dimension, and yet your feelings have so much to teach you.

When working with Sevens in leadership, it is important to listen to how they communicate. The entertaining stories of adventure do include aspects of what they are feeling; tune in to these things. If you force them to connect at a feeling level, or if you force them to be serious about things that make them feel trapped, they will work harder at finding escape than at doing what you need from them. In connecting to their energy and enthusiasm, try to find small ways where their feelings show up and honor those moments of balance.

Eights

The doing dominant Eights can be bigger than life as they demonstrate a strength and confidence not seen in any other type. Eights engage the world through the doing dimension and focus on being productive and on protecting themselves. Their energy seems boundless as they automatically respond to life with gut-level responses doing the things that are most important to them. They want to make sure they are not being controlled or manipulated in their work and want to maintain their own sense of power in what they do.

In terms of their stance, maintaining power and control leads to easily dismissing the feelings of others as well as their own (see Figure 7.8). The fear of being betrayed means that Eights are not interested in vulnerability, but they have to learn that a gentle connection as a leader is not weakness. It is actually a strength and is essential to effective leadership.

The wake-up call that Eights must learn to identify is the belief that they must push and struggle to make things happen. Eights sense within themselves a bitterness and frustration with others in work-related situations.

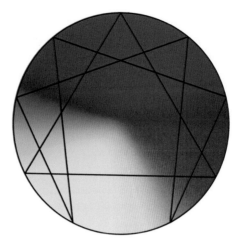

FIGURE 7.8 Eights: How does the intensity of pushing through keep you from recognizing how others feel?

This can lead to social isolation and a desire to just do things on their own. A lack of empathy comes with this struggle and sometimes a sense of rage. The passion of Eights that develops from this is known as lust, or intensity. It is an externally focused anger as opposed to the One's internal focus. It is a struggle with control and the desire to be in charge of one's own situation.

Eights move against what gets in the way of the pursuit of their agenda. Eights do not want to be controlled by others. They want to do what they believe needs to be done in the world. They have a gut-level response that says, "You are not the boss of me" (or at least that is what my wife loves to say!). And, they move against whoever or whatever is perceived as trying to control them.

As leaders, Eights feel the sense of anger they carry, but they must develop comfort with other feelings. To do this, you can practice listening deeply to a few others whom you trust. Listen to the impact you have on them in helpful and harmful ways. Listen to how you communicate and notice how assertive it feels to others. Can you allow others more control in your work together? This does not have to mean letting them control you, but allow yourself to be affected by them and observe when anger is the response you feel. Can you acknowledge that feeling? Can you look within to observe and notice other feelings?

If you lead with or supervise an Eight, you likely already know better than to try to control how they approach their work. But do they feel controlled? Do they feel trusted? Do they feel they can trust you? It is important to be honest with Eights, so tell the truth about what they need to know about their work. Talk about how your work together affects you. When there is conflict, be clear and concise and don't expect a response. Say what you need to say and then get back to work; do not expect an Eight to process their work relationship with you. Even if they do not show it, know that your care matters and so does your commitment to trust in the work you are doing together.

Threes

As with Sixes and Nines, Threes are the final number who have the same dimension that is dominant and repressed. Threes recognize the feelings of others, they worry about how people feel about them, but Threes do not sit with feelings long enough to take them into account when they respond to the people around them (see Figure 7.9).

This demonstrates the common experience that Threes are more comfortable with doing and thinking than feeling. In addition, Threes in leadership are typically focused on their own plans and action. They strategize a vision for their work and make a plan to complete it.

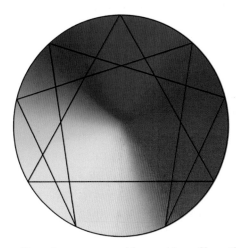

FIGURE 7.9 Threes: How does your need for seeking affirmation and attention from others keep you from nurturing authentic connection with them?

They are efficient, hardworking, and committed to what is best for themselves and the organization.

Again, Threes care about the organization's success because they want to be loved by the people within it. However, they are not always aware of what it really means to connect in a loving, feeling way. Stancewise, this is because Threes also repress feelings. As Stabile says, "Threes are personable, not personal." I recently attended a marketing workshop that actually encouraged this as a strategy: "Be personable, not personal." For some types, this may be a skill to learn in order not to be so driven by feelings, but to engage a more doing orientation. For Threes who operate this way at their core, the opposite is needed. Threes must engage at a feeling level, making emotional connections, and being vulnerable in the workplace.

This feeling connection must be developed and it must be genuine. From the perspective of being feeling repressed, Threes believe personal connections are too much work, at best and at their worst, they get in the way of meaningful work. However, Threes are also feeling dominant so they want the value of connection and relationships. The result: Threes too often fake a feeling connection to appear emotionally connected. "Fake it 'til you make it" does not really work at an emotional level and the result is a disingenuous way of engaging others.

The wake-up call for Threes is this inherent drive for status and attention. Threes want to avoid a sense of shame if their work were to appear unsuccessful, so they push to create an image of success thinking their value depends on it. This creates anxiety, another feeling to be avoided. It creates burnout and an emptiness within. The expectations for achieving success are unrealistic. This reinforces the passion of vanity, proving a worth that is neither genuine nor realistic.

Threes move against what gets in the way of the pursuit of their goals. They are focused on success and accomplishment. They are pragmatic and efficient. And they push against whatever interferes with their need to achieve. However, at times, it is their pushing against and their lack of connection that prevents the success they so desire.

If you are a Three in leadership, you are likely aware of the ways you desire relationships while also avoiding them. Seek to put relationships before tasks as a part of your work routine at some point in your day. When you do stop to connect, allow the relationship to be genuine. Strive to be truly personal in your connections.

If you are leading with a Three, support the relationships they invest in at work. Don't call them out for not being genuine; they likely know this is the case. And don't be patronizing in your recognition of their personal connections. Offer praise for their work, for what they accomplish, and offer praise for the ways they support colleagues and seek to connect. Support their feeling efforts as well as where they excel in thinking and doing, and this will encourage them to appreciate this balance that is needed.

ADJUSTING YOUR STANCE

For each Enneagram type, and across the three stances, we have seen the ways feeling, thinking, and doing are out of balance, and ways to bring them into balance. The repressed dimension plays a significant role in creating this lack of balance we each have in our personality. You have seen some ideas for adjusting in order to develop the repressed center. This can be described as work that helps you to adjust your stance.

Adjusting an assertive stance means nurturing feelings and engaging the heart in empathic leadership.

Adjusting a dependent stance requires developing an objective lens and engaging the head in open-minded, big-picture leadership.

Adjusting a withdrawing stance includes an active body engaged in the work that is required for effective leadership.

It sounds simple enough. And yet, for none of us is this shift quite so straightforward. We must make these moves and we must learn to adjust our stance, but the first steps are rooted in mindful awareness. Now we turn to several steps that are of value for all nine types as we recognize what it takes to adjust our stance.

CHAPTER EIGHT

STANCEWORK
Developing Balance for Leadership

One of my best friends, Meghan, identifies as an Enneagram Two. She really identifies with being feeling dominant and how she is driven to do something as she engages others at a feeling level; however, she does not love the idea of being thinking repressed. On the other hand, she does understand what this approach to self-awareness can teach her. She realizes the way the three centers are out of balance within her. In fact, she has known the Enneagram for over a decade and identifies stances as the most practical element of the Enneagram. "The work of the Enneagram is stancework," she tells us. What does that mean? It is the way we engage the three dimensions of our personality as we to seek to balance them.

In talking with us about these things, Meghan had this to say: "The big piece of awareness for me is to recognize that I don't always focus on my thinking. I do think so often with my feeling and doing that I need to pay attention to the ways that I don't really stop to think. For me, it takes being alone, slowing down and practicing more thinking. I create a mental image of a boundary between my head and my heart and then I try to focus on the thinking side of things."

We asked what this means for Meghan as a leader. The question was to get her thinking! And she knew it. Meghan added: "I'm going to lead with my heart and I'm going to lead by creating connection with you. What I have learned is this cannot be the only way I lead. I have to make sure that I'm a balanced leader instead of just one shaped by feeling and doing."

She is a great leader, and a truly intelligent one. She leads the care team at our university, a team of case managers who provide resources and connections for students in crisis. As part of her work recently, she had to create annual goals and use data to benchmark them. Her response to this task: "I feel more exhausted by all of that work than if I had met with eight students in crisis." She later thought to herself (and then texted me): "I have worked so hard today, and it's only lunch. I've had so many days with much harder work, but not like this!"

Being thinking repressed is not about intelligence as much as it is subconscious preferences for the heart and hands over the head. Meghan identifies with being a solution-focused and feeling-oriented campus leader. She values being a supervisor and loves her time with students. And she is great at it. How can Meghan learn to trust and value her critical thinking and the depth of knowledge she holds in the same ways that she knows herself to be a feeler and a doer?

This kind of reflective questioning is the internal leadership development task I call stancework. Earlier I discussed the importance of growing our soul, of seeking balance in our soul. Stancework is the commitment to seeking balance in the three dimensions of your personality to grow our soul, to develop our full potential. It is grounded in a recognition of the three Enneagram dimensions we have considered: Which is most dominant for your personality, which supports the dominant dimension, and which dimension is repressed? Stancework is not a matter of a quick fix for one's personality. Stancework begins with the recognition of the ways we regularly live our lives with these elements out of balance and then discerning what it takes to bring the dimensions into balance.

In fact, while we may now see the imbalance of these dimensions in our personality, most of us like the ways we have learned to function and don't know that we want to fix or change anything. We at least find comfort in the patterns of who we have become. We may be able to see the flaws in it. We may know our Enneagram passion and see how it affects us. However, we also see the strengths of our personality and we are not sure that this change is worth the work.

Meghan knows the way that thinking is the repressed dimension of a Two. She knows that this results in a dependent stance where she relies on others to help her make decisions and think through big questions. But she also knows that she is loved for how attuned she is to people's feelings. There is no denying that strength of connection and relationship at the core of everything she does. Meghan sees how she overrelies on seeking connection and nurturing relationships. It is how she functions most comfortably. Some would even say it is who she is. She would say it is who she has been for most of her life, but it is not all of who she is.

STEPS IN STANCEWORK

Meghan and I have been having these conversations for over a decade. She still knows the ways in which her personality is dependent and I am just as aware of how assertive I can be. And yet, we have seen so much change within us. We are better leaders now than we were then. We have learned to practice self-observation in nonjudgmental ways. And this is step one in soul growth.

Observing personality at work in the world is step one, followed by *listening* to what we can hear about our way of working from others and from within, and finally by *allowing* time and energy for the slow work of change. These are the elements of awareness and transformation, away from the personality that has been engraved on us and toward the essence of who we are called to be. These are the essential components required for the internal work that is the foundation for more effective externally-focused leadership.

Leadership by the numbers means knowing your number, but the Enneagram is so much more than a number. Knowing your number provides you with some basic information about yourself. Knowing which of the three stances describes your way of being in the world provides a deeper level of Enneagram knowledge. Enneagram wisdom is learning to sit patiently with these things as you observe your life, listen to the details of who you have become, and allow a renewed sense of self to emerge. And, in this, you will become the leader you want to be.

Step One: Observe

An Enneagram practice associated with the work of Gurdjieff has come to be known as nonjudgmental self-observation. It is a practice that takes some work. We live in a world where *judgmental observation* is a part of everyday life. Everywhere we turn we hear, "Can you believe that. . . .", "I can't stand. . . .", or "I'm so glad I'm not. . . ." We also practice *judgmental self-observation* pretty well: "I will never. . . .", "I am so. . . .", or "I can't possibly. . . ." *Nonjudgmental self-observation* is different. It still provides critical, even painful, insights, but the nonjudgmental element is essential. It means that we must learn to hold lightly (rather than tightly) what we observe within ourselves. We must remain honest about our self-reflection and the insights that we are developing; however, we must learn to be gentle with ourselves as we discern what they mean.

Asking "what" we observe and avoiding "why" questions can help with this. "What" questions invite us to consider new ways forward as we seek to acknowledge, accept, and allow what we see in ourselves. If we start with "why" questions, we never get to the bottom of our search:

Why am I this way?
Why do I do the things I don't want to do?
Why can't I change this about myself?

These lead us to reflect in ways that are tangential to what is happening in the present moment. They reinforce beliefs and stereotypes that may or may not be helpful. They lead us to over-identify with certain assumptions we hold about ourselves rather than honest observations of what is happening within us in the present moment.

"What" questions help us pay attention to the details of what we are experiencing in the here and now. These can include:

What do people see in me as I lead?
What do I see in myself?
What are the ways I have engaged my feelings today?
What have I done to repress them?

These can help us identify less with constructed images we have of ourselves that may or may not be true.

In writing about self-observation, organizational psychologist Tasha Eurich says, "'Why' questions trap us in our past; 'what' questions help us create a better future." We fool ourselves with the answers to why. We present an overly optimistic response or an overly pessimistic one. Explaining why something has happened or is the way it is was shown to be less helpful in Eurich's research than developing insight about new ways forward: "'Why' questions trap us in that rearview mirror. 'What' questions move us forward to our future" (Eurich 2018).

What can you observe within yourself in this moment?

What elements of your number and stance are shaping you today? And over the past week?

What is the pattern of thinking, feeling, and doing that is out of balance?

Ask these questions. Observe what is there in the present moment. Hold the reflections lightly and without criticism.

Honest observation without harsh judgment takes work and requires patience. Here are some thoughts and questions to consider for practicing nonjudgmental self-observation based on each of the three stances.

Stancework Reflections for Nonjudgmental Self-Observation

A way to engage in nonjudgmental self-observation is to set aside intentional time to reflect on the ways your personality shapes your leadership on a given day or during a given week. Each day this week, stop and ask yourself the questions for your stance. And make sure you spend some dedicated time with your responses. Can you do this for 10 minutes at the end of your day?

> For *Assertive Stance* leaders: How are doing and thinking driving your approach to your work? What role do feelings play? Are you fully considering the feelings of others? What are you feeling today? Are you able to create the time and space for your own feelings? To do so requires slowing down. How easy is that for you given the way you approach your leadership? Are you comfortable nurturing an open heart as you lead?

For leaders in the *Dependent Stance*: How are feeling and doing pervasive in the ways you go about your work? Are you aware of the emotional weight that you carry as a leader? That is the intersection of feeling and doing, and while you may spend a lot of time asking questions, talking through options, reinforcing ideas that are important to you, this overthinking is not the same as having an openness to your thinking. What are some new ideas you have about your work? What are new ideas you have heard from others? What plans can you make for these ideas? What creative or original ideas do you have today? How do you foster an open mind as you lead?

For *Withdrawing Stance* leaders: How are you locked in to feeling and thinking? And while the energy you invest in reflection and analysis seems like doing something, what tasks and activities have you set aside to accomplish? What more needs to be done? How can you prioritize things differently with an openness to engaging your body? What do you see others doing? How are your colleagues exerting energy in their work? What are you doing today that really needs to be done? Can open hands help you lead in new ways?

Step Two: Listen

The ancient Chinese word for *listen*, transliterated as *ting,* means to completely hear something with your whole body, or as one translation offers, "to hear with your heart as well as your head." Chinese words often build on other words, and that is true here. *Listen* incorporates the word for "undivided attention" as well as "eyes," "ears," and "heart." This suggests a difference between the concept of hearing and listening. Hearing is the act of sounds coming to our ears; listening is the attention we give to what we hear. The beauty of the Chinese word also includes a focus on undivided attention to what is being heard so that all the senses taken in can be fully engaged.

Listening as a part of Enneagram self-reflection requires an openness to hearing something new and different about ourselves. It means hearing something from the perspective of heart, head, and hands. A common misunderstanding of the Enneagram is that it reinforces stereotypes we have of ourselves, that it limits our ability to see and hear. Listening, however, is less about what you believe about yourself as a type Four, or as an assertive stance, or as a thinking-centered leader; it is more about asking what you notice happening within yourself as you make your way through each day.

Eurich describes self-awareness as "the meta-skill of the 21st century" because it is foundational to all of the skills that are required for effective leadership. She presents two approaches to self-awareness, internal and external. Internal self-awareness has to do with listening from the inside out. She describes "an inward understanding of your values, passions, aspirations, ideals, patterns, reactions, and impact on others. People who are high in internal self-awareness tend to make choices that are consistent with who they really are, allowing them to lead happier and more satisfying lives" (Eurich 2018).

External self-awareness is listening from the outside in. She writes, "Because externally self-aware people can accurately see themselves from others' perspectives, they are able to build stronger and more trusting relationships. Those low in external self-awareness, on the other hand, are so disconnected with how they come across that they're often blindsided by feedback from others."

The growth of our soul requires listening from within and without. It includes hearing with our eyes, ears, and heart. It is an undivided commitment to being aware of how we function in the world. Our Enneagram stance shapes how we function in the world and so we must ask: What we can hear about ourselves from the perspective of our stance? And are we listening to what we hear? Rumi said, "the quieter you become, the more you can hear" (Rumi and Barks 1996). How is that true for us from the perspective of our stances? Consider these questions:

➤ Assertive stance types, are you listening to people's feelings from a nurturing perspective?
➤ Dependent stance types, are you listening to thoughts and ideas in a wholistic manner?
➤ Withdrawing stance types, are you listening to what is required of you, to what needs to be done and when?

Step Three: Allow

One of my favorite memories from seminary was one of the most challenging and one that took the longest to learn—the practice of contemplative spirituality. Dr. Glenn Hinson taught these courses and he started every class with a contemplative prayer, a form of mindful meditation. He would often invite us to "allow ourselves to open before God like a flower opens to the morning sun." The phrase was so synonymous with his teaching that a stained-glass window was created in his honor symbolizing a person opening as a flower to the sun.

What does it mean to allow ourselves to be open in this way? Whether or not you identify as a Christian, or with any faith tradition, there is value in the practice of learning to allow. In learning to be open in new ways. Enneagram wisdom implies an openness to change and that openness is the outgrowth of listening and observing as we have described them. How does change happen? Not by force. Not with a list of new strategies or principles, but rather an approach to self-awareness and to openness to change. We know that what brought us to the place where we are now in life will not take us where we want to go. What new thing must we be open to, what must we allow, in order to seek balance in our lives?

The word *allow* implies possibility and opportunity rather than force or imposed will. Dr. Phil, Phil McGraw, made popular his notion that "willpower is a myth." He goes on to say, "The problem with trying to use willpower to achieve and sustain a behavioral change is that it is fueled by emotion. And as we all know, our emotions are, at best, fickle. They come and go. When your emotions start running down—and they will—even your best-laid plans will fall flat" (McGraw 2020).

We have learned that relying only on emotion can be a setup for failure. However, the same is true for relying only on strength or only on intelligence. The wisdom of the Enneagram is that we need the emotional insight of the heart, the instinctive strength of our hands, and the intelligence of the head to bring a balanced perspective to what motivates us. As we have seen, we are too often motivated by one of these dimensions and we too often underrely on another. By learning to see the value of all three, we learn not to force change in our lives. We learn that we need more than a traditional approach to willpower. We need balance and we must learn to be open to the slow, steady insights that will bring change.

What new opportunities associated with Enneagram awareness related to the stances can you identify? How will they nurture balance? The work associated with stances begins with a posture of self-reflection, guided by nonjudgmental self-observation and the practice of listening to what our lived experiences are teaching us. From here, stancework moves to allowing change to develop within. Once we learn to see the ways the three dimensions of the Enneagram are out of balance in our lives and which of the three dimensions is most repressed within us, we can allow work associated with the repressed center to develop within us.

As we have noted, assertive stances must allow a renewed openness to the value of feelings in their lives, dependent stances to the role of thinking, and withdrawing stances to the importance of doing. We must each be open to the development of these dimensions in a new way. Put another way, assertive stances require open hearts, dependent stances can attend to open heads, and withdrawing stances can nurture open hands.

OPEN HEARTS: HOW DO FEELINGS MATTER?

The assertive stance types, the Threes, Sevens, and Eights, have inherently learned to see the value of doing and thinking. Stancework requires their openness to the role of feelings. They must learn to ask themselves what they are feeling. And, they must be more attuned to the feelings of others. They must learn to do so in a sustained way. As an assertive stance myself, I admit that I know the importance of feelings, but that is not the same thing as being open to feeling them in the moment when they are happening. I want to be in charge of when I attend to feelings. Developing a true openness to the role of feelings means being open to them in real time, as they occur, when we or someone with whom we work is expressing them.

When I teach this in a workshop, someone usually remarks that feelings don't belong at work. Or, that some people are so feeling dominant that their feelings get in the way and that we can help correct that. Perhaps these things are true; however, there are many times when assertive stances are pushing against feelings because we are uncomfortable with them and not because they are inappropriate in a given moment.

A leadership framework associated with the role of feelings in leadership is that of emotional intelligence. Emotional intelligence focuses on the recognition and regulation of our own feelings in our interactions with others and on empathy and support for the feelings of others. What experiences make us anxious and afraid? What stirs sadness and shame within us? How do we sense hope and joy? As well as grief and loss? Are we able to notice these things? As they are happening? Can we stay with these feelings? Each of them? In real time?

Emotional intelligence requires a shift from skills and intellect alone, from intelligence (IQ) and technical prowess, to self-knowledge that allows oneself to see what affects our moods and what motivates us. This shift of attention points to social skills rooted in empathy and compassion. Goleman, Boyatzis, and McKee, in their book *Primal Leadership: Unleashing the Power of Emotional Intelligence* list self-awareness as a key element in emotional intelligence and explains it as the ability of a leader to recognize how their feelings affect them and to recognize the feelings of others. They say we can, and must, learn to develop empathy, to "internalize empathy as a natural response to people" (Goleman, Boyatzis, and McKee 2013). They add that empathy does not get much respect in the business world, but that it is responsible for the organizational success of some of the most effective and well-known leaders.

To develop emotional intelligence is to develop self-awareness and empathy. To take next steps in our development as assertive stance Enneagram types is to practice emotional intelligence (EQ). It is to learn to feel one's own feelings and attend to the feelings of others. The work here is learning to open our heart, and this is always the most difficult task for assertive leaders. As we move against, as we look to the future, as we analyze and plan for success, how can we also learn to observe, listen, and allow feelings to guide us in more open-hearted ways?

To help us with the work of self-awareness, I invite you to revisit the Enneagram image for the assertive types. Remember, the red represents feeling; the yellow, thinking; and the blue, doing. What is the color and dimension least present in these images? How does that reflect your life and your leadership if you are one of these types? How does your team need more connection to feeling? How are you nurturing relationships? Developing emotional intelligence? Take some time to reflect on the image for your type and how it represents you (see Figures 8.1 through 8.3).

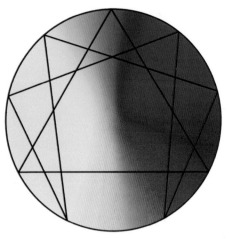

FIGURE 8.1 Enneagram Seven.

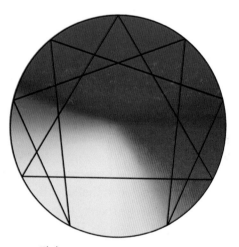

FIGURE 8.2 Enneagram Eight.

After reflecting on your Enneagram image, consider how to practice these ideas as you learn to open your heart:

- Make time to visit with your staff for a few minutes each day and learn about their personal lives.
- Practice more active listening. Make a note of what you are hearing from others and avoid focusing on what you want to say in response.

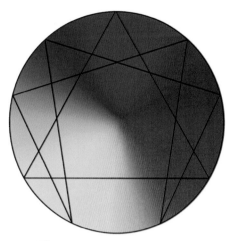

FIGURE 8.3 Enneagram Three.

- ➤ In addition to your "to do" list, find a list of feeling words and identify three feelings each day that arise in relation to your work.
- ➤ Simply notice the ways you were attentive to feelings and the moments when you could have been more attuned to feelings. Don't judge yourself; just notice.

OPEN HEADS: HOW DOES THINKING MATTER?

In 1939 at Holyoke College, Dr. Walter Kotschnig told students to keep their heads open, "but not so open that your brains fall out." He criticized students who go to college merely to learn a skill and urged his listeners to find the "real aim of education, to acquire a philosophy of life, intellectual honesty, and a constant search for truth" (Kotschnig 1940). These are words of wisdom for all of us. An invitation to an open mind, to opening our heads, is particularly of value for people in the dependent stance as their focus is more on right action and relationship, with a desire for right thinking, but with a tendency to rely on one set of ideas or beliefs rather than an openness to multiple ways of thinking.

Ones, Twos, and Sixes like to think of themselves as thinkers; however, they often have a stronger preference for what is right versus what is wrong. A clearly decided-on right and wrong can be helpful, but sometimes such an approach prevents an openness to multiple ways of thinking, multiple ways of seeing things. Ones want what is good, Twos want what is kind, and Sixes want what is loyal, and once they have decided what is good, kind, and loyal, it is not easy to dissuade them. We all tend to default to dualistic ways of thinking, and that is truer for this stance than the others. Learning to consider multiple perspectives, to foster an open mind, takes time and energy that may delay the right response they have decided on.

Developing a nondualistic way of thinking refers to more diverse and dynamic ways of reflecting on life and life's opportunities. Richard Rohr (2011) has been a proponent of nondualism as a spiritual way of engaging life's challenges. An African approach to nondual thinking is known as "diunital thinking," and it is a way of thinking that seeks to consider how two or more ways can be considered equally as part of a single whole. In coining the term that is grounded in African thought, Vernon Dixon said that "diunital ways of thinking" ask us to consider "something apart and united at the same time" (Dixon 1970).

Making sense of a world that can be understood for its parts as well as its whole is a challenge for any of us. It is easy to find ourselves experiencing a full mind, an overwhelmed mind, and it is more difficult to nurture an open mind. It is more difficult to learn to quiet our minds.

What are the ways we must learn to see the good and the bad in someone at the same time? To pay attention to what we do know and to be open to what we have yet to learn? It may not only be the dependent stance types who wrestle with this; however, it is the case that this group is prone to engage doing and feeling more than thinking. For dependent stances who have a tendency to move with others, how can you observe, listen, and allow yourselves to think in more open ways?

To help you practice self-awareness, revisit the Enneagram image for the dependent stance types. Remember, the red represents feeling; the yellow, thinking; and the blue, doing. What is the color and dimension least present in these images? How does that reflect your life and your leadership if you are one of these types? How does your team need more connection to thinking? How are you nurturing critical, independent thinking? Developing nonduality in your thinking? Take some time to reflect on the image for your type and how it represents you (see Figures 8.4 through 8.6).

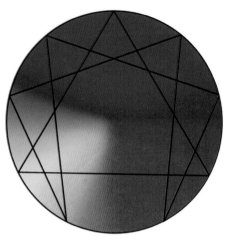

FIGURE 8.4 Enneagram One.

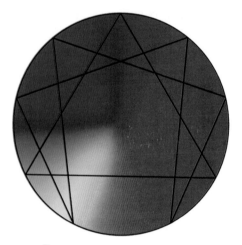

FIGURE 8.5 Enneagram Two.

After reflecting on your Enneagram image, consider how you might practice these ideas as you learn to quiet your mind:

- ➤ Read a work of nonfiction and share with someone what you are learning.
- ➤ Pay attention to a conversation where you have the tendency to reinforce a belief or opinion you have. If you are hearing a perspective different from your own, make a note of when someone offers a

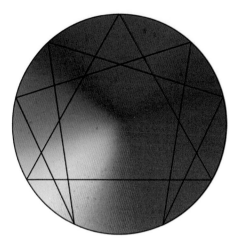

FIGURE 8.6 Enneagram Six.

perspective different from yours that you disagree with and consider
how their view has value. You don't have to adopt their view; just
consider its value.

➤ In addition to your "to do" list, make a list of "to read" and find one new
online source that introduces you to a new idea each day. Set aside
15 minutes to read it without any intention of sharing it with someone
or immediately doing something with what you learn.

➤ Simply notice the ways you were attentive to thinking and the
moments when you could have been more attuned to opening your
mind in new and different ways. Don't judge yourself; just notice.

OPEN HANDS: HOW DOES DOING MATTER?

Polish math scholar Jacob Bronowski valued knowledge for the way
it leads to action: "The world can only be grasped by action, not by
contemplation." Human hands are instruments of discovery. They
are unique resources that work with the human mind to foster our
creativity, and Bronowski believed that neither could allow us to develop
knowledge without the other. He went so far as to say, "The hand is more
important than the eye. . . . The hand is the cutting edge of the mind"
(Bronowski 1973).

Educators know that in order to make learning meaningful for children
we must foster a passion for learning with arts and crafts, cooking,

music, and gardening. While having truly distinct learning styles may be an educational myth, tactile or kinesthetic learning is the "hands-on" approach to learning that incorporates touching and doing.

It can be said that Fours, Fives, and Nines trust their hearts and their heads more than their hands. The use of our hands as a symbol for doing invites withdrawing stance types to be more engaged, to be more hands on. They have to learn to see the value of their hands in the same ways they trust their heart and head. Too often, withdrawing stance types assume that the time and energy they invest in thinking and feeling is productive doing. Because these numbers invest more energy in thinking and feeling, they have to remember and trust the value of taking action. They have to learn the value of their active and engaged contributions.

Moving from idea to action was central to the W.K. Kellogg Foundation's creation of logic models in the 1980s to help community organizations develop programs that could be evaluated for their effectiveness. In teaching nonprofit leaders to connect their mission with concrete programs their agencies offer, they often struggled to develop effective strategies that were able to be implemented. Logic models ask: Can organizations move from ideas and resources to activities that yield outputs and outcomes? Many organizations offered innovative ideas, but could they offer effective action in their communities? Logic models helped create specific, achievable tasks that leaders could implement.

Withdrawing stance leaders get the logic part of this model. They enjoy making plans; implementation can be the challenge. Withdrawing types must be able to ask what their priorities are. And they must ask what others expect of them. What are the tasks that I need to accomplish? And by when? Having concrete plans makes it more likely for a doing repressed personality to put their ideas into action. For withdrawing stances who have a tendency to move away from what is required of them, what leads to action? How can you observe, listen, and allow yourselves to do in more open ways?

To help you practice self-awareness, revisit the Enneagram image for the withdrawing stance types. Remember, the red represents feeling; the yellow, thinking; and the blue, doing. What is the color and dimension least present in these images? How does that reflect your life and your leadership if you are one of these types? How does your team need more connection to doing? How are you learning to implement your ideas in concrete, meaningful ways? Taking action in order to be present and to do what is required of you? Take some time to reflect on the image for your type and how it represents you (see Figures 8.7 through 8.9).

After reflecting on your Enneagram image, consider how you might practice these ideas as you learn to engage your strength:

> ➤ We mentioned how other stances need more than a "To Do" list. For withdrawing stances, creating an actual daily "To Do" list that is feasible for you is a good first step.

FIGURE 8.7 Enneagram Four.

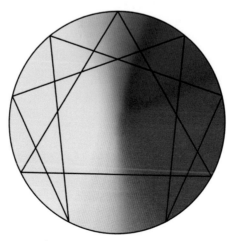

FIGURE 8.8 Enneagram Five.

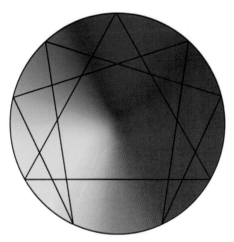

FIGURE 8.9 Enneagram Nine.

- In promoting physical fitness, people are encouraged to take small steps. A good beginning is going for a short walk. Use short walks as a way to engage your body and encourage movement and action.
- Identify an accountability partner for bigger projects. Who is someone who can work with you or meet with you on occasion to report progress on important tasks?
- Simply notice the ways you were attentive to doing and the moments when you could have been more attuned to taking action. Don't judge yourself; just notice.

This chapter begins to point us within—to the inner work required for external leadership. From these questions that nurture self-awareness, we are prepared to take even more significant steps for the inner journey. The next chapter provides such steps to help us begin to see the need for balance in our lives even more clearly.

CHAPTER NINE

ESSENTIAL PRACTICES FOR DEVELOPING BALANCE FOR THE INNER JOURNEY

Conscience calls me to be myself.
To be myself begins with self-knowledge.
Self-knowledge begins with work on myself.
Work on myself is based on the sensation of myself.

—Jean Vaysse (2009)

For some of our personalities, we are learning the importance of tuning in to emotions and to feel our feelings. These assertive types need to focus on the heart center. For some, it is more a matter of turning to our mind, creating a curiosity and openness to ideas. Dependent stances are those who need a renewed attention to the head center. And some need to focus on tasks. Their withdrawing need is tied to their hands and their mantra could be the classic, "Don't just sit there, do something."

However, each of us can find great value in the reverse of this mantra. Many of us have heard the play on words with this opposite challenge, "Don't just do something, sit there." It's a clever take, but do we ever really try it? Literally?

Try it right now. For 45 seconds. And take several deep breaths. Count to five as you breathe in and count down from five as you breathe out. Take five deep breaths. This is the start to a practice that can truly calm your body. These breaths engage the vagus nerve and the parasympathetic nervous system, helping you to relax, and calming anxiety. They help bring balance to heart, head, and hands. Del Negro, Funk, and Feldman (2018) have gathered much of the scientific research in their paper, "Breathing Matters," where they remind us of the connection between the physical act of breathing and the emotional and cognitive factors that influence our breath. Feeling, thinking, and doing both influence our breathing and our ability to breathe deep is influenced by these three dimensions.

Before we can learn to breathe, maybe we need to learn to sit. Jean Vaysse was a mid-20th-century French surgeon and a follower of the teachings of Gurdjieff. In *Toward Awakening*, he describes how he has learned that "we live in self-forgetfulness, and it happens without leaving any trace. Life lives itself, but there is no fruit for the one who has lived it." Overcoming our automatic habits is not about doing something that makes us more busy. It simply requires the difficult task of sitting. Yes, sitting. In learning to sit, we develop skills for self-observation, listening, and allowing. He writes, "As I become more able to see myself, the inadequacies and failures that I record no longer arouse regret or impulses to correct myself." He presents the struggle of learning to sit, "An exercise of this kind has no meaning unless it is connected each time to our need to become a little more ourselves." His book, which tries to clarify the esoteric and mystical writings of Gurdjieff, includes an entire chapter on learning to sit still in order to observe, listen, and allow.

In order to sit, we need a place to rest that is comfortable. Any seat will allow us to fill the connection of our legs, our bottom, and parts of our back. A chair that allows your feet to feel the floor works better in that it allows you to be grounded (more on that later). Notice your body in the chair, what fills your mind, and what emotions get stirred. Try not to chase the thoughts that fill your mind, the anxiety of your body, or the feelings that stir in response to others. Notice these things. Then let them go. Focus on yourself, your breath, and your body. Sit. And notice you are sitting. Just sit. Only focus on sitting. Let everything else go. Soon, you will realize just how difficult it is to do nothing and just sit there. Can you do it for 10 minutes? 3 minutes? 45 seconds?

Now that you not only know your number, but know the value of increased self-awareness, you can begin to understand the importance of developing practices such as this for self-reflection. Our minds are distracted. Our bodies are fidgety. Our hearts are overwhelmed. We then respond to these challenges of life with automatic reactions of our personality. The needs of our ego lead us even as we consider ourselves to be leaders.

Learning to observe your personality, to listen to the ways it shapes your leadership, and to allow enough grace and compassion to develop new ways of being takes a commitment to developing new practices. Here, I introduce several practices to help you tune in to the three core dimensions that shape your Enneagram type, stay out of balance, and perpetuate the struggle of our personality. We call these practices mindfulness, but they connect us to mind, heart, and body in new and important ways.

MINDFULNESS PRACTICES

Many of the practices I am encouraging here and much of my perspective on the Enneagram is rooted in the practice of mindfulness. I deeply value centering prayer, similar contemplative spiritual practices, and forms of meditation that help us empty our mind and find the deep quiet within us. Each of these practices has similarities to practicing mindfulness. Mindfulness is, in many ways, simpler to practice and can be practiced in very short periods of time. Actually, any period of time where you commit to being aware of the present moment is a mindful practice.

Mindfulness has been around in many forms for millennia, particularly in Asia given its Hindu and Buddhist roots. Jon Kabat Zinn created Mindfulness Based Stress Reduction, drawing from Eastern sources. Among those was Thich Nhat Hanh, whose work has been a gift to my own understanding of these things. Connecting the practices to Christian traditions, Tony De Mello taught "awareness," and Thomas Keating taught centering prayer. The benefits of mindful practices have been demonstrated over and over again. Since the early 1980s, dozens of studies have been conducted to show how mindfulness reduces anxiety and alleviates some symptoms of depression. These practices are integral for our health and well-being.

Are you willing to take some time to sit and observe what you are feeling in the moment or to pay attention to all of the thoughts and feelings that are cluttering your mind right now? Doing so is essential for Enneagram reflection and is a mindful practice. How do I develop a mindfulness practice? The following discusses four mindfulness practices that can be incorporated into your Enneagram reflections as a way to observe, listen, and allow—as you seek to develop greater self-awareness.

Grounded Present Awareness

The first makes sense to those of us who are educators. We know the importance of grades and a grade point average (GPA). I want to suggest a different way to think of a GPA: Can you develop grounded, present awareness? This simple acronym can remind us to be mindful.

What does it mean to be grounded? Can you experience a connection to the ground? To your chair? To your body? As you breathe, where do you feel your breath? Only in your nose and mouth? Can you feel it in your chest? Can you sense your torso rising as you breathe in? And can you feel it release as you breathe out? Take a few minutes to breathe, to connect your breath and your body, and to be grounded in the place where you are alive and well.

And then, what does it mean to be present? As you breathe, as you feel yourself breathing, pause and be still in the present moment. You are alive in this moment and all shall be well. We may not know what the future holds, but we can breathe and be grateful that we exist in this present moment.

Finally, can you be aware of what is happening as you are grounded and present? What do you see? Smell? Sense? Allow yourself to simply experience with genuine awareness all that surrounds you right now. Take it in.

To nurture grounded, present awareness is to be mindful. Being mindful is essential to see our personality more clearly and foster a sense of balance. As educational leaders, we are so focused on what is coming next. We master the art of juggling multiple expectations. We seldom slow down. Even as you read, you are likely aware of the mountain of responsibilities waiting on you. Before you move on, recognize that awareness you have of your business as a leader. As part of your commitment to reading this chapter, take a few minutes to reread and reflect on these questions as you seek to be grounded, present, and aware in this moment.

Mindfulness Moments

Another way to learn to slow down and be present is to create a series of mindfulness moments each day. This series of exercise takes less than a minute each, three times a day. It is simply a matter of pausing throughout your day to focus on your breathing as you seek to be grounded in the moment.

Here's how I came to practice it. Several years ago, a fellow associate dean set a timer each hour on the hour. When it chimed, he would pause and take three deep breaths. And then continue with his work.

I doubted I would practice this each and every hour, but wanted to try something. Suzanne Stabile had once encouraged a group of us to pause and observe our personality at a few set times throughout the day. I thought this might be a time to try it.

How often and when would I pause? As I considered this, another question came to my mind: When is the best time to drink Dr Pepper®? The advertising campaign from 1924 told us it was at 10 a.m., 2 p.m., and 4 p.m., times of the day when our sugar levels drop in between meals. So, being a loyal Dr Pepper® drinker (it originated near Waco, Texas, don't you know?), I set timers on my phone to pause at 10 a.m., 2 p.m., and 4 p.m. daily.

My goal is to pause and take three deep breaths when the timers go off. In all honesty, there are several times throughout each week when I shut the timer off and do not stop to reflect or take deep breaths. I just power through! But in the moments when I do stop, it always seems worth it. Just last week, I was with a gathering of friends and a 4 p.m. timer went off. I was tempted to ignore it and keep going. My daughter was in the room and she said, "Dad, is that your breathing timer? Everyone, let's stop and take three deep breaths." I was grateful for her willingness to model this for us!

At each moment you choose to set aside, sit still and take a few deep breaths as you ask yourself: How am I paying attention to the importance of feeling? Of thinking? Of doing? As a leader, the tasks of the job are endless. And they show up over and over again each day. As part of the busy-ness of your work, can you turn some attention to yourself each day? If you are not ready for multiple mindfulness moments each day, start with two minutes as you are getting ready to leave for the day. Start with an end-of-the-day practice of looking back on the day and asking about the role of feeling, thinking, and doing in your day.

Welcoming Prayer

You may see the value of mindfulness and you may consider yourself to be a praying person. A particular approach to mindfulness in prayer that Father Keating taught was known as the welcoming prayer. It is an invitation to welcome whatever life presents us and in recognizing life's pain in the moment, we can welcome these experiences for use in our healing. The prayer is a mindfulness-based meditation that calls us to welcome all things, and also to let things go. It is hard enough to welcome what comes our way. And it is just as difficult to let these things go.

Keating is teaching us to let go of our desire to change life's situations. More specifically, he calls us to let go of our desire for power and control, our desire for affection and approval, and our desire for security and survival. Even if you are not religious or spiritual, consider how these words might guide you as a meditation. Below is a version of the welcoming prayer written by Mary Mrozowski for you to consider:

> Welcome, welcome, welcome.
> I welcome everything that comes to me today
>   because I know it is for my healing.
> I welcome all thoughts, feelings, emotions, persons,
>   situations, and conditions.
> I let go of my desire for power and control.
> I let go of my desire for affection, esteem,
>   approval and pleasure.

I let go of my desire for survival and security.
I let go of my desire to change any situation,
  condition, person or myself.
I open to the love and presence of God and
  God's action within. Amen.
  (Mrozowski and Keating 2017)

Knowing that the desire for power and control are inherent struggles for Enneagram doing triad types; that the desire for affection, esteem, approval, and pleasure resonate with feeling types; and that the desire for survival and security are central to thinking triad types, I wrote an Enneagram version of the welcoming prayer. In place of these three desires, I list the Enneagram desire for each of the nine types. You may identify most with the desire of your type, or you may find some resonance with several of them; regardless, I hope you find value in the slow recognition and release of the desires that keep us distracted and on auto-pilot. My hope is that this language, this practice, can be an additional resource for your self-reflection as a leader.

Welcome, welcome, welcome.
I welcome everything that comes to me today
  because I know it is for my healing.
I welcome shame, fear, and anger.
I let go of my desire to be good, and to have integrity at all costs,
I let go of my desire to feel loved in every interaction,
I let go of my desire to feel valuable and worthwhile,
I let go of my desire to be uniquely myself, to find and express
personal significance,
I let go of my desire to be capable and competent,
I let go of my desire to find support, guidance and security,
I let go of my desire to be happy and fulfilled,
I let go of my desire to protect myself,
I let go of my desire to be at peace and experience wholeness,
I open myself to the love and presence of God and
  God's action within. Amen.

Reciting the prayer is a helpful place to begin. However, the prayer involves more than a focus on the words. The words are an invitation to mindful reflection. Pause with each line as you read it. After each "welcome" take a deep breath and let yourself welcome and accept, allow, whatever is filling your heart or mind in that moment; welcome it.

In addition to welcoming what you are carrying, the prayer includes an invitation to let these things go. Letting go of deep desires rooted in the passion of our personality does not happen easily. We have to learn to see these desires at work within us. It is only in recognizing it and observing how it is at work within us that we can let go of it. Can you see your desire? Do you see the ways it affects your leadership? Does it prevent you from being the leader you hope to be? My desire to feel valuable often gets in the way of making hard decisions. It prevents me from being as attuned to the details as I need to be. I am too often more committed to proving my worth than doing the highest quality work. I can welcome this. And I can let it go.

What is your desire? Can you recognize the ways your leadership is tied to an inherent desire we all have to be in control of whatever situation comes our way? To experience the support and approval of our colleagues for how we lead? To have a sense of safety and security in our work environment? For each of us, one of these lines from the original prayer may be more clearly motivating for you.

Maybe the desires of the revised prayer resonate more with how you feel in your leadership role. Is one of these nine, each associated with an Enneagram type, something you are aware of as you lead? We all want to be happy. We all want to be loved. We all want to be competent in our role. However, does this desire function at a level that drives the decisions you make or the ways you approach your colleagues?

As we have seen, Riso and Hudson describe how these desires drive our personality types. So much so that the desire of our personality too easily deteriorates into the worst version of our personality, particularly if we are not willing to slow down and practice self-awareness, including some form of reflection like this prayer. Here is what that list looks like for each type:

> Ones have the desire for integrity, which deteriorates into critical perfectionism.
> Twos have the desire to be loved, which deteriorates into the need to be needed.

> Threes have the desire to be valuable, which deteriorates into chasing after success.
> Fours have the desire to be oneself, which deteriorates into self-indulgence.
> Fives have the desire to be competent, which deteriorates into useless specialization.
> Sixes have the desire to be secure, which deteriorates into an attachment to beliefs.
> Sevens have the desire to be happy, which deteriorates into frenetic escapism.
> Eights have the desire to protect oneself, which deteriorates into constant fighting.
> Nines have the desire to be at peace, which deteriorates into stubborn neglectfulness.
> (Riso and Hudson 1999)

Can you recognize the desire and the way it deteriorates for your type? When you begin to see this happen, can you recognize it? Can you welcome it? Can you release it? This is the inner work of the welcoming prayer as a mindful tool for developing your best self and a path for growth as a leader. My hope is that this practice might call you to slow down and to look within.

Image-Based Meditation

Lydia Fogo describes an opportunity for inner work that we can use with the Enneagram image. She writes, "Art's ability to keep us fully engaged in the present moment is likely the main reason engagement with the visual arts can cultivate mindfulness" (Fogo 2017). While much of her focus is on creating art, the practice of being present to an image is an invitation to reflect mindfully on your experience and approach to leadership.

Take a moment to revisit your Enneagram stance image from Chapter 6 and compare it to the balanced image of the Enneagram in Figure 9.1. What is the difference? How do you see your life reflecting your type and stance rather than the balance of the dimensions. Rather than reading these questions and moving on, pause for 5–10 minutes and practice the image-based meditation below.

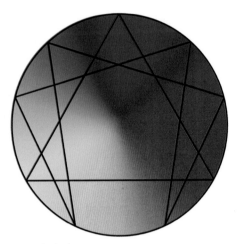

FIGURE 9.1 Enneagram in balance.

Enneagram Image Mindfulness Meditation

Take a moment to find a comfortable place to sit. Sit with your back straight in an upright position, rest your hands in your lap, and feel both feet as they connect to the floor.

Now take three deep breaths in and out. Breathe in slowly and breathe out even more slowly.

As you continue to sit and breathe, notice your body. What are the sensations as you sit? Are there any places of discomfort? Any places where you feel tightness? Or tension? Notice any feelings you may be experiencing? Are you carrying anxiety? Grief? Frustration? Do you feel these feelings in your body? Try to identify where you feel them. Sit for a few moments with your feelings and in your body.

As you continue to sit, notice what fills your mind. Is it busy? Jumbled? Are you making To-Do lists? Are you distracted by what is next on your agenda? By a focus on other people? Sit with and notice all that is running through your mind. Don't dwell on what is there, and don't push it away. Notice it and then, as though it were a cloud in the sky, let the ideas float on by. Return to your body and your breath.

Now, are there connections you can make between what is in your head, with what you are feeling emotionally, and with how you feel it in your body?

As you sit with these dimensions, focus on the image associated with your Enneagram type and the preceding balanced image. First look at your Enneagram image. What primary color is least present in it? What does that mean for you? How is that reflective of your day? Of how you are leading this week? Now look at the balanced Enneagram image. How does the presence of the colors here compare? How can you focus more on feelings and the need for red? On thinking if you need more yellow? On blue if you are doing repressed?

Spend a few minutes comparing the images and sitting with what this means for you. Try not to over-analyze the images. Just notice what comes up for you. Stay in this moment.

After several minutes of reflection, take three more slow, deep breaths. Then allow yourself to move around as you return to your day.

Our educational contexts demand more from us each and every year. The challenges are greater and the resources are fewer. The opportunities are more exciting and yet the energy is less available. And if you do not feel these things, your team certainly does. In order to find a new way to lead, we have to develop a sense of balance in terms of how we approach our work, and I am convinced that this begins by looking deep within ourselves.

The practices in this chapter are essential for slowing down, for looking within, and for developing balance. Trusting your gut cannot be your only tool. Your analytical skills will take you only so far. Building relationships is not the answer to all your questions. Learning the ways you lean and what dimension needs to be developed is the way to becoming the leader you long to be. Knowing your number is step one, but the gift of the Enneagram is an invitation to balance as you lead. The power of heart, head, and hands is where wisdom for your leadership can be found.

Before we turn to the next chapter and focus more externally on how we lead our organizations, consider what commitment you can make to using these mindful practices as part of your leadership development.

CHAPTER TEN

ESSENTIAL PRACTICES FOR DEVELOPING BALANCE FOR THE OUTER JOURNEY

The critically acclaimed film *The Assistant* follows Jane, a well-educated, underemployed office assistant through a day in her new job and begins with a half hour of almost no dialog. It is simply Jane making her way through a day in her office. It becomes clear she works 24/7 for a boss that everyone tiptoes around though he is never seen in the film. With little real dialogue in the film, the characters say very little about the company's culture; however, the film still has plenty to say about it nonverbally. The toxicity of the bureaucracy in this office's organizational culture is clear.

What is organizational culture? It is often said that it is difficult to define, but easy to experience. Ravasi and Schultz define it as the shared assumptions in our organization that guide our behaviors and shape our experiences (Ravasi and Schultz 2006). It includes such things as the beliefs, values, assumptions, perceptions, traditions, actions, norms, thoughts, and feelings of our workplace.

Actions, thoughts, and feelings all make the list. In other words, doing, thinking, and feeling help define our workplace. Flamholtz and Randle (2011) teach that organizational culture is the personality of our organization. Externally, we communicate organizational mission, vision, goals, and objectives; these reflect internal value, relational, and power dynamics. Likewise, as leaders, we may express external statements about who we are and how we desire to lead, but as we have seen, these reflect internal dynamics of our capacity for feeling, thinking, and doing.

How do we lead in such a way to promote a healthy organizational culture? Like most things, it is not something that happens automatically, but something that takes intentionality. It requires a mindful approach to leadership. It requires an awareness that the Enneagram can help foster. It means we must slow down enough to consider how our automatic responses and reactions to everyday situations reinforce the habits of our personality and of our organization's culture.

Father Rohr describes how our automatic reactions fail to create the culture we desire. He writes, "the opposite of contemplation is not action, it is reaction" (Rohr 2013a). His Center for Action and Contemplation is committed to how mindful contemplation and action-oriented leadership work together. To skip the work of mindfulness in hopes of the more action-oriented leadership skills only reinforces the reactive patterns of our personality and of a negative and harmful organizational culture.

I hope it has become clear that the automatic responses of our personality are examples of reactive leadership. Every time I force a decision, it is the reactive leadership of my assertive personality at work, my doing-thinking team that leaves out feelings, and it is not the kind of effective action orientation I genuinely desire. My "moving against" is perhaps most clearly recognized as a reactionary approach, even though I often choose to describe my style as strategic or visionary. These words may describe the ideas I put forth, but my style, when I fail to connect to feelings, is still reactive. As assertive stance leaders, we must continually learn to open our hearts.

We see reaction in the assertive types, but we can also recognize it in my dependent stance leaders who always want more opportunity to check with their colleagues before deciding. It may be more kind than the assertive approach, but it is no more effective. Just as the assertive leaders must slow down, the dependent stance leaders must work to clarify the ideas in their own mind in real time and be prepared to act on them. Their "moving with" has its value, but for them is an automatic response that fails to fully engage the thinking dimension that is essential for effective leadership. Dependent stance leaders must continually learn to open their heads.

This is also true in the withdrawing stance leaders who prefer thinking and feeling to action. Their reaction may be inaction, but it is still an automatic response that they must learn to recognize. "Moving away from" may help them preserve energy in the moment, but it does not lead to effective and active leadership. Withdrawing stance leaders must continually learn to open their hands.

Riso and Hudson teach us that "by relaxing our bodies, quieting the chatter of our minds, and allowing our hearts to be more sensitive to our situation, we open up to the very inner qualities and resources that can help us grow" (Riso and Hudson 1999). This is, of course, more difficult than it sounds. The inner journey practices of the last chapter are designed to help us practice the observing, listening, and allowing that is required if we want to open our hearts, heads, and hands in new ways. These practices help us develop the wisdom needed to balance the three centers of intelligence, the three Enneagram dimensions of our personality. These practices nurture mindfulness, and as a result, help us find the balance we need to lead.

How, then, do we take those inner practices and turn them into effective action? How do they help us slow down our reactive approach to leadership rooted in personality and develop a more centered and balanced approach that is active in a healthy way? How do we practice these things in an effort to lead effectively and nurture healthy organizations? To help us recognize our reactive approach to leadership and to bring it to bear on our organizational culture, I believe there are specific lessons that come with developing our repressed center. For assertive leaders to connect with feelings is to cultivate community. For dependent leaders to trust their thinking and that of others is to nurture confidence. For withdrawing leaders to act in ways that value a commitment to doing is to foster creativity. Let us consider each of these lessons that reflect the work of the three stances.

THE PRACTICE OF COMMUNITY: LESSONS FOR ASSERTIVE STANCE LEADERS

Assertive leaders who are able to nurture the role of feelings can also nurture connection and community in their work. Observing how they cut off connection to their own inner life and the emotions of others, listening for the meaning that comes in the depth of relationships, and allowing change transforms the experiences of Threes, Sevens, and Eights into leaders guided by kindness and compassion. Rather than a forced or artificial connection, authentic community is the experience when these leaders slow down enough to be present with others.

As a Three, I know the painful truth of rushing past people to focus on results. An Eight leader I know describes being focused on productivity over process. I work with other assertive leaders who care deeply about the people on their teams but struggle to show it. We recognize the weight of emotions and wrestle with them, learning to nurture an open heart in our work.

The doing and thinking team is perhaps most aware of its repressed center and its struggle to make sense of the importance of the heart center in our leadership. We trust the doing and thinking combination that drives our work. Feelings are messy and uncertain. We do not easily understand them and certainly cannot control them. Learning to balance our drive for ideas and action with the important work of EQ is our challenge. Reflection on these things can encourage us to trust the value of relationships in our leadership. Below I will break it down by the numbers in this stance.

As assertive stance leaders, we can recognize the importance of this shift as we learn to value relationships at work and recognize feelings in ourselves and others. According to Hurley and Donson, strengthening this feeling connection points to the highest purpose of this dimension: "to hear the dignity in every human heart and perceive the deeper reality in people" (Hurley and Donson 1993). They point to human growth, development, healing, and renewal as the resources for fostering community that the heart dimension nurtures in our work.

Developing personal relationship and expressing your emotions in a life-giving way is the gift of the feeling dimension and essential for healthy community building.

THE PRACTICE OF CONFIDENCE: LESSONS FOR DEPENDENT STANCE LEADERS

For dependent stance leaders, thinking independently can inspire confidence as it reflects an openness to new ideas, trust in themselves and others, and a willingness to set limits where needed. Observing how they are reluctant to think in new ways, listening to the voice that offers reassurance, and allowing change transforms these types into dynamic and self-assured leaders. For Ones, Twos, and Sixes, this is not the second-guessing or reinforcing of a previously held view, it is not an opinionated or self-deprecating expression of an idea, but rather leadership reflective of an open mind and engaging their head to share their perspective with confidence drawn from critical reflection.

I have mentioned my leadership team with several dependent stance leaders. Our school needs their voices, and we need to hear their bold vision for our work together. In other schools, I know leaders in this stance who embody a feeling and doing approach with a repressed thinking dimension. They are as smart as anyone and that may be quite clear, but they may struggle to seek and trust guidance from within, or to be open to new or different ideas if they have strong opinions about something.

The doing and feeling combination results in underdeveloped thinking for Ones, Twos, and Sixes. Recognizing their propensity for overthinking rather than the space for a quiet mind can help them practice an openness to new perspectives and a trust in their own. Ones who feel responsible also feel resentful, and share their wrestling with their need to be right. Twos who also feel a burden of responsibility in the level of care they provide talk about learning to see how much they worry about disappointing their colleagues. Sixes catch themselves asking questions, but worry that they might not ask a question that is needed to make their big decision. In hearing these, most of us comfortably recognize the ambiguity of life and accept that we cannot live up to all the expectations. As dependent stances wrestle to develop this openness, they see the value in new ways of thinking even when it is uncomfortable.

In this, a life of confidence is nurtured for these leaders. They learn to value the trustworthiness of information about themselves or their situation. They learn to appreciate the perspective that can be gained by taking time to look at the big picture. Living by faith is a hard lesson for any of us, but the balance these leaders desire nurtures trust and confidence in themselves and others. Below I will consider this for each type in this stance.

In these leaders, we begin to see the importance of elevating the thinking dimension to bolster their sense of confidence and more meaningful connections as they lead. For Hurley and Donson, nurturing the thinking dimension is still relational; it means learning to trust. In this stance, the big picture seems overwhelming and their approach to making sense of it may not feel trustworthy. A myopic view gets reinforced where hard facts are preferred over the world of gray that shapes so much of what we see as we lead. In learning the value of seeing beyond black and white, dependent stance leaders achieve balance by seeking more information and new knowledge. They recognize that the highest use of the thinking dimension is confidence in the ability to develop clarity of vision while recognizing the complexities of life. The confident development of a personal vision for your life is the gift of the thinking dimension.

THE PRACTICE OF CREATIVITY: LESSONS FOR WITHDRAWING STANCE LEADERS

For leaders in the withdrawing stance, where doing is the repressed center, a focused action yields creativity and an enlivened engagement of the practical needs that surround them. Observing their inner struggle to act, listening to what is needed of them, and allowing change can be transformative for these leaders. A reflective life need not be a withdrawing life, but rather can be a life committed to the engaged and effective use of their doing center that yields creative action. This is not the reluctant action with which Fours, Fives, and Nines are familiar, but a dedicated focus on open hands and an engagement of their body center to act in new and creative ways.

Where do we see this? A friend in the withdrawing stance is department chair for one of the most successful academic programs in our university. Another has served at the highest levels of leadership.

I know leaders who are Fours, Fives, and Nines and who are successful deans and directors. Their leadership styles reflect the traits we describe in looking at the thinking-feeling team that is doing repressed. They are slower to act than I am in almost every situation; they are also more committed to a thoughtful, deliberate response than I am.

In talking to these leaders, I hear their recognition of preferring feeling and thinking to doing. Learning to see and hear where they are not fully engaged fosters change. A Four describes how they want to be in the right mood before they act. A Five shares how they need to really understand something to exert the energy required of them. And a Nine says they have to really believe something is worth doing to muster the inner resources to act. However, when they reflect in this way, they all comment how recognizing the imbalance inspires action and a desire for balance.

What I see in these leaders are the principles of creativity coming to life. Hurley and Donson describe creativity as a commitment to hope. To "imagine a future filled with hope" means trusting the energy that is available to them and the ways it can help them contribute to positive change in their environment (Hurley and Donson 1993). "I want people to know they can depend on me," one leader says. "I want to do all I can for the sake of my students," another offers. And, finally, we hear, "My colleagues desire and deserve my very best." Below I look at what this means by the number.

The purpose of the doing center is what withdrawing leaders are learning to identify in new ways. These purposes are movement, action, and intention. Balance in the three dimensions is experienced when these leaders recognize the difference they can make in the world, and the positive ways they are able to influence and inspire others. This creative engagement helps these thoughtful, reflective leaders work for change, to do what is good and right in ways that are grounded in their natural commitment to thinking and feeling. Actualizing your ideas and plans in the world is the creative gift of the doing center.

BACK TO CULTURE

As we each identify our repressed center and nurture its true purposes in our personality, we learn to balance the three dimensions within us and lead in a more healthy and holistic manner. Recognizing what we can offer in terms of the practice of community, confidence, and creativity are vital to our leadership within an organization and the culture we help foster.

We know the challenges of the outer journey all too well; how we approach these challenges is what matters most. We may know what needs to be done but fail to develop the relationships needed for the work, know how people feel but do not have a vision or trust in our own leadership to act decisively, or have all the right ideas but lack the creative energy to implement a way forward. The wisdom of the Enneagram shows us that we fail to balance the three dimensions that make us truly human. From an unhealthy imbalance we wobble forward, learning to recognize the call of the Enneagram to wake up to the imbalance that keeps us fractured within and keeps our teams, schools, units, and organizations from being the best we can be.

An emerging theme of my school and in social work education is the concept of anti-oppressive practice. As we seek to address racism from an intersectional perspective, our faculty want to consider each of the elements of identity that keep people marginalized and that prevent us from being the inclusive school that results in equity and belonging for each of our staff, faculty, and students. Left to the patterns of my personality, I will struggle and push against the prejudice and bias that still show up in our work, and in my desire to make sure I am valued, I too often fail to see my own privilege at play; I am blind to the ways my power and position can reinforce the status quo. While I am pushing, my team wants to slow down and check in with colleagues as we make big decisions. We are busy and we are tired, so it takes time and the time spent getting everyone on board can perpetuate the inequities within our school.

One recognition we have is that we have created a nice culture. Writing about cultures of niceness in *Harvard Business Review*, Timothy Clark cautions against a culture where we avoid conflict and maintain comfort, but at a cost to colleagues whose voices represent difference and diversity. The pursuit of consensus is not full inclusion and this creates ambiguity and indecisiveness. The "low-velocity decision-making" that is the result of nice culture encourages everyone to go along to get along (Clark 2021). It keeps us on auto-pilot, operating out of the habits of our personality, rather than discerning what else is needed to become more healthy in our work together.

Recognizing where tension and difference exist can result in a culture that values kindness more than niceness. My leadership team is striving to create a culture that is kind. "Clear is kind" we often say, but we often settle for nice. Perhaps we need to be more honest and forthright. We need to encourage more space for candor and confrontation. To do so will demand the best of our work together as we seek to practice community, confidence, and creativity. It will require the openness of heart, head, and hands. We know the Enneagram in our school and can do more to assure that every person is valued and represented. And even more importantly, we can do more to develop the feeling, thinking, and doing dimensions of each type, of each person.

Let's revisit the numbers and consider how reflecting on the work of our stances can help us be more effective as we develop as leaders and enrich connection with others. Based on what we know about the stances and the need to bring our Enneagram dimensions into balance, let's consider how we might feel, think, and act in new ways as a result of pausing to pay attention to the culture of our organization. The result will be more effective teams, more meaningful responses to the people with whom we work, and a deeper sense of authenticity within ourselves.

As educational leaders, the following questions can contribute to a stronger sense of identity for you as a leader and a stronger culture for your school or organization. Paying attention to personality is essential for fostering a culture of connection. To do this, we have to learn to pay attention to what captures our attention. Notice what you see in the world and how you see it. Notice how your colleagues see the world differently. The ways they see are different and they truly see different things. What do you see?

Assertive Stance: How can you cultivate feelings for what you see?

Sevens look around and see new ideas and opportunities. Noticing options creates freedom and flexibility. It also prevents full engagement in the present moment and limits connections required for a deep sense of community. Before you share your ideas with others, watch and listen to your colleagues more intently. Who do you need to listen to more fully today—without thinking about what you want to say next? This opens a feeling-based connection.

For Eights, staying in control of a situation hides vulnerability. It also prevents community building. You have an impulse to act that is often self-protective. What are you protecting? What do you feel under the gut-level response to act? This may not feel like the strength to which you are accustomed, but it is not a sign of weakness. You may not think you need others, but this might help you see otherwise.

Threes see their work and their tasks. Everywhere they look there is something to do. They are creative and visionary in a way that focuses on roles they play that lead to accomplishment. What value do you have apart from these tasks? Who are you apart from the tasks? A heart-centered question to ask is: What is the source of my identity? (And don't let the answers focus on the things you do.) Knowing who you are helps you know how to support connections and community more authentically.

Dependent Stance: How can you think critically about what you see?

For Ones, you see what is right and what is wrong. Notice how you evaluate, correct, judge, form beliefs and opinions, criticize, reform, and improve. What else can you see? What is good and right in the response of others? And in yourself? This can represent a shift in thinking, thinking more broadly about possible paths toward what is good. Seeing the good in others and yourself will strengthen your relationships with your team.

Twos see people and connections. Even when reading nonfiction, a Two may be thinking about who they can share their new ideas with. How can you step away from a focus on others to time spent truly on yourself? What is self-care that doesn't involve someone else? What are the inner experiences you can nurture? These shifts invite thinking about yourself and your needs in a new way and will ultimately result in more authentic confidence and wholehearted connection.

Sixes take in everything and come up with questions as they go. You naturally see what can go wrong; take some time to try to notice what is problem free. What has the potential to go well can be a new way of thinking. Instead of connecting through questions, this can lead to confidence and clarity as you connect with others.

Withdrawing Stance: How can you connect action to what you see?

Fours want connection with others and desire to draw that connection from within themselves. You see an interior world that you long to authentically engage as you connect. Can you connect with a greater focus on the qualities of others? Allow yourself to see something meaningful within yourself. Then, without comparing, notice something of value in someone else. You are inherently creative; let this lead to creative action as you engage others as you lead in new and meaningful ways.

For Fives, knowledge comes more easily than connection. You take in so much about others without having to exert the energy of relationship. Insert yourself as part of your team; look at them, not as part of observing your environment, but as part of relationships that strengthen your work. What can you say or do to share what you know? How can you ask for the input of others as you prepare to act on your ideas?

Nines want to reinforce positive regard and want to avoid problems and tension in their connections. They see everyone else's perspective, but lose sight of their own. Think of something that is important to you and ask for it. Then listen to the ideas of others. How does your work together require an active sharing of different perspectives? Nines are called peacemakers; how can you do the work of negotiating differences as you lead? How can you ask for support from your team for the work you are committing to do?

A wide range of responses is needed from us as we lead diverse organizations with different goals and purposes. We know this about our work and we are learning to know ourselves, yet we struggle to consider all that is needed from us as we easily slide back into what comes most naturally. In light of Enneagram differences, knowing our stance provides the most practical guidance for what we can do differently—for how we can be different.

Cultivating feelings helps assertive types build community.

Thinking critically helps dependent stance leaders develop confidence.

Action is required for a withdrawing leader to be their best creative self.

Leading with these things in mind also helps to build the culture we desire in the organizations in which we lead. To lead in new ways, to develop strong teams and thriving organizational cultures, we need to see ourselves, our capacity for leadership, as clearly as possible. To take the steps and act on the questions suggested in this chapter, we absolutely need the mindful practices of Chapter 9. To lead the people around us, we must look within in a new way. The Enneagram's invitation to recognize the imbalance of the three dimensions at the core of your leadership can help pave the way forward for you.

Suzanne Stabile founded Life in the Trinity Ministries as the home for her Enneagram teaching. The group's motto is that this is individual work that cannot be done alone. As leaders, we each must learn to value self-awareness and find a way to strive for balance within. We must also learn to work together as we seek to grow and become our best selves. The well-being of our souls depends on it. The health of our leadership requires it. The success of our organizations demands it.

EPILOGUE

The first paragraph of the Introduction to this book took me back to a meeting at the end of a long day where I was not fully present. I was in the meeting. I was actually leading the meeting. But I was not grounded and aware in the present moment. I was there, but I was distracted by a need to please people and woo people and look successful as I rushed through that meeting and on to the next one.

Last week I was in another long meeting at the end of a long day (at the end of a long semester). I was leading a discussion of three curricular proposals that were controversial in our school. The curriculum committee had spent months on these, and I knew there were a wide range of thoughts and feelings about each item on the agenda. The first two items had been tabled the month before and now they were back on the agenda but with enough buy-in to pass almost unanimously. The third item was much more controversial. More people had more feelings about it, and even though there had been several discussions with key stakeholders, we did not have consensus. I called for a vote on the item and there were more yeas than nays, but also more abstentions than usual. There was not a true tie, but nor was there a clear majority in support of the measure. I wanted my academic leadership team that had been working on the proposal to feel good about the outcome—and my leadership—and I knew the group would not be. I wanted the faculty members who raised questions to feel heard—and to feel good about me—and this was also not going to be the case. Have you noticed the theme of me worrying about how people feel about me?

After taking my time to count the votes, I paused. I took a deep breath. I knew I would upset people who were ready for this to move forward and those who had wanted to shut this down, but decided it was worth it. I was present to myself. I was present to the struggle at hand. I was present to how my colleagues felt but did not let that dictate my decision. I asked the committee to spend more time on the proposal and to bring it back for further discussion and a vote at a later date. This kind of decision can be described as putting off an inevitable difficult decision, as kicking the can down the road; however, no one took it this way. The committee and my academic leaders knew it would take additional hard work, but to most everyone, it felt worth it. And to those who were frustrated, that is okay.

In this moment I did feel confident about my decision. It did not feel easy. I let myself feel that. I let myself feel the frustrations. I let others feel their frustrations. In the end, taking time to make the difficult decision felt right.

I am seldom willing to make unpopular decisions. A 360° review several years ago pointed out that I avoid difficult decisions for fear of upsetting people. As a Three, I am aware of being this way, but not always aware enough in the moment to make a different decision. I am not always mindful enough to weigh other people's responses and then to let those outweigh my need for comfort and support.

The Enneagram helps me see these things more clearly. Enneagram stancework reminds me of my worry about how others feel about me and of my need to pay attention to a host of feelings in more meaningful ways as I lead. Observing myself takes time, takes energy, and takes courage. When I rush it, I observe only a sliver of what is true, and my self-observing is far too judgmental. Nonjudgmental self-observation is the key to being the leader I want to be. Listening to my own needs and listening more carefully, intentionally, to the needs of others is also key to my leadership growth. Observing and listening, and sitting in the moment, led me last week to the right decision for our school. Sitting in that moment led me to suggest our sitting together longer. In the end, we knew sitting a while longer was the right thing to do.

Adam Grant (2022) recently tweeted: "Personality is not your destiny. It's your tendency. No one is limited to a single way of thinking, feeling, or acting. Who you become is not about the traits you have. It's what you decide to do with them."

As you reflect on your leadership, I hope the journey of self-awareness becomes more intentional and more focused. As leaders, we like to think we are self-aware, but there is always more to see within. And we seldom, if ever, spend enough time in that mindful space of observing and listening to the extent that is needed. We try to change, but don't allow the space and time to allow new ways of being to develop. May this book be a reminder of the value of this kind of work. May it give you new insights for your own leadership. And may it be a resource for lasting change and transformation, and the growth of your soul into the leader you long to be.

REFERENCES

Allport, G. (1960). The open system in personality theory. *The Journal of Abnormal and Social Psychology* 61(3): 301–310. https://doi.org/10.1037/h0043619.

Arons, A., van den Driest, F., and Weed, K. (2014). The ultimate marketing machine. *Harvard Business Review* 55–63. https://hbr.org/2014/07/the-ultimate-marketing-machine.

Bradberry, T. & Greaves, J. (2009). *Emotional Intelligence 2.0*. San Diego, CA: Talentsmart Press.

Brooks, K. (2018, April 12). M.C. Escher's Relativity. https://moa.byu.edu/m-c-eschers-relativity.

Bronowski, J. (1973). *The Ascent of Man*. Boston: Little, Brown and Company.

Brown, B. (2012). *Daring Greatly: How the Courage to Be Vulnerable Transforms the Way We Live, Love, Parent, and Lead*. New York: Penguin Press.

Campbell, J. (2012). Nine paths: Exploring the highways and byways of the Enneagram. https://ninepaths.com/stance-keyword-checklist/.

Clark, T. (2021). The hazards of a "nice" company culture. *Harvard Business Review*. https://hbr.org/2021/06/the-hazards-of-a-nice-company-culture.

Del Negro, C., Funk, G., and Feldman, J. (2018). Breathing matters. *National Review of Neuroscience* 19(6): 351–367. doi:10.1038/s41583-018-0003-6.

Dixon, V. (1970). The di-unital approach to "Black economics." *The American Economic Review* 60(2): 424–429. http://www.jstor.org/stable/1815840.

Dotlich, D., Cairo, P., and Rhinesmith, P. (2006). *Head, Heart, and Guts: How the World's Best Companies Develop Complete Leaders*. San Francisco: Josey Bass.

Doyle, G. (2016). *Love Warrior*. New York: MacMillan.

Eurich, T. (2018). *Insight: The Surprising Truth About How Others See Us, How We See Ourselves, and Why the Answers Matter More Than We Think*. New York: Penguin Random House.

Flamholtz E., and Randle, Y. (2011). *Corporate Culture: The Ultimate Strategic Asset*. Stanford University Press.

Fogo, L. (2017). Engagement with the visual arts increases mindfulness. University of Tennessee, Honors Theses.

Goleman, D. (1995). *Emotional Intelligence: Why it can matter more than IQ.* New York: Random House.

Goleman, D., Boyatzis, R., and McKee, A. (2013). *Primal Leadership: Unleashing the Power of Emotional Intelligence.* Boston: Harvard Business Review Press.

Grant, A. (2022). [Twitter] 2 August. https://twitter.com/adammgrant/status/1554 490823429001216?lang=en.

Hanh, T.N. (2002). *Anger: Wisdom for Cooling the Flames.* New York: Penguin Random House.

Heifetz, R., and Linsky, M. (2002). *Leadership on the Line: Staying Alive through the Dangers of Leading.* Brighton, MA: Harvard Business School Press.

Hollinger, D. (2005). *Head, Heart, & Hands: Bringing Together Christian Thought, Passion and Action.* Colorado Springs, CO: IVP Books.

Horney, K. (1950). *Neurosis and Human Growth.* New York: W. W. Norton.

Hurley, K., and Dobson, T. (1991). *What's My Type? Use the Enneagram System of Nine Personality Types to Discover Your Best Self.* New York: Harper San Francisco.

Hurley, K., and Donson, T. (2000). *Discover Your Soul Potential: Using the Enneagram to Awaken Spiritual Vitality.* Lakewood, CO: WindWalker Press.

Hurley, K., and Donson, T. (1993). *My Best Self: Using the Enneagram to Free the Soul.* New York: Harper One.

Ichazo, O. (1982). *Interviews with Oscar Ichazo.* Kent, CT: Arica School.

Keating, T. (1999). *The Human Condition: Contemplation and Transformation.* Mahwah, NJ: Paulist Press.

Kotschnig, W. (1940, January 27). Professor tells students to open minds to truth. *Blytheville Courier News.* Blytheville, Arkansas.

Labanauskas, J. (2021). A tale of two Enneagram branches. *Enneagram Monthly* 258.

Lubbe, J. (2020). *The Brain-Based Enneagram: You Are Not a Number.* Dr. Jerome D. Lubbe.

Mandela, N. (1995). *The Long Walk to Freedom.* New York: Back Bay Publishing.

McGraw, P. (2020, April). https://www.drphil.com/videos/i-cant-stop-my-son-from-eating-too-much-says-dad-of-650-lb-man/.

Mezirow, J. (2000). *Learning as Transformation: Critical Perspectives on a Theory in Progress.* San Francisco, Jossey-Bass.

Mrozowski, M., and Keating, T. (2017). Welcoming prayer, *Contemplative Outreach.* https://www.contemplativeoutreach.org/welcoming-prayer-method/.

Naranjo, C. (1994). *Character and Neurosis: An Integrative View.* Nevada City, CA: Gateways.

Nicoll, M. (1996). *Psychological Commentaries on the Teaching of Gurdjieff and Ouspensky. v. 3.* Newburyport, MA: Red Wheel/Weise.

O'Hanrahan, P. (2019, August). Moving on the lines. https://theenneagramatwork. com/moving-on-the-lines.

Palmer, P. (2000). *Let Your Life Speak: Listening for the Voice of Vocation*. Hoboken, NJ: John Wiley & Sons.

Pargament, K. (1997). *The Psychology of Religion and Coping: Theory, Research, Practice*. New York: Guilford Press.

Pugh, K. (2011). Transformative experience: An integrative construct in the spirit of Deweyan pragmatism. *Educational Psychologist* 46(2): 107–121. doi:10.1080 /00461520.2011.558817.

Quirolo, L. (1996). Pythagoras, Gurdjieff and the Enneagram. *Enneagram Monthly* 14–15. http://www.enneagram-monthly.com/pythagoras-gurdjieff-and-the-enneagram.html.

Ravasi D., and Schultz, M. (2006). Responding to organizational identity threats: Exploring the role of organizational culture. *Academy of Management Journal* 49(3): 433–458.

Riso, D., and Hudson, R. (2003). *Discovering Your Personality Type*. Boston: Houghton Mifflin.

Riso, D., and Hudson, R. (1999). *The Wisdom of the Enneagram*. New York: Bantam.

Roderick, L., and Merculieff, I. (2000). *Stop Talking: Indigenous Ways of Teaching and Learning and Difficult Dialogues in Higher Education*. Anchorage: University of Alaska.

Roeser, R. (2020). Educating the head, the heart and the hand in the 21st century: Notes from India and the United States. UNESCO Report. https://mgiep. unesco.org/article/educating-the-head-the-heart-and-the-hand-in-the-21st-century-notes-from-india-and-the-united-states.

Rohr, R., and Ebert, A. (2001). *The Enneagram: A Christian Perspective*. New York: Crossroad.

Rohr, R. (1995). *Enneagram II: Advancing Spiritual Discernment*. New York: Crossroad.

Rohr, R. (2011). *Falling Upward: A Spirituality for the Two Halves of Life*. San Francisco: Jossey-Bass.

Rohr, R. (2013a). *Silent Compassion: Finding God in Contemplation*. Cincinnati: Franciscan Media.

Rohr, R. (2013b). *Yes, And . . .: Daily Meditations*. Cincinnati, OH: Franciscan Media.

Rumi, J., and Barks, C. (1996). *The essential Rumi*. San Francisco: HarperCollins.

Simon, H. (1957). *Models of Man: Social and Rational*. New York: Wiley.

Singleton, J. (2015). Head, heart and hands model for transformative learning: Place as context for changing sustainability values. *Journal of Sustainability Education* 9. http://www.susted.com/wordpress/content/head-heart-and-hands-model-for-transformative-learning-place-as-context-for-changing-sustainability-values_2015_03/.

Soosalu, G., and Oka, M. (2012). *mBraining: Using Your Multiple Brains To Do Cool Stuff*. mBIT International.

Stabile, S. (2018). *The Path Between Us*. Downers Grove, IL: Intervarsity Press.

Taylor, E. (2017). Transformative learning theory. In: *Transformative Learning Meets Bildung*. (eds. A. Laros, T. Fuhr, and E.W. Taylor). International Issues in Adult Education. Rotterdam: SensePublishers. https://doi.org/10.1007/978-94-6300-797-9_2.

Thompson, C. (2015). *The Soul of Shame: Retelling the Stories We Believe about Ourselves*. Downers Grove, IL: InterVarsity Press.

Usher, S. (2017). *More Letters of Note: Correspondence Deserving of a Wider Audience*. Edinburgh, Scotland: Canongate.

Vaysse, J. (2009). *Toward Awakening*. Morning Light Press.

Williams, A. (2020). Preparing for reality: Bringing Together the Head, Heart, and Habits. Washington, DC: National Council on Teacher Quality. https://www.nctq.org/blog/Preparing-for-reality:-Bringing-together-the-head,-heart,-and-habits.

INDEX